WRITING TO THE POINT

WRITING TO THE POINT
SIX BASIC STEPS

William J. Kerrigan

Fullerton College

 Harcourt Brace Jovanovich, Inc.

New York   Chicago   San Francisco   Atlanta

Library of Congress catalog card number: 73-14127
ISBN: 0-15-598310-5

Printed in the United States of America

TO THE INSTRUCTOR

If you're searching for a method of teaching composition that over a period of twenty years has proved itself successful with thousands of regular and remedial students in community colleges and universities—a method that starts from scratch and teaches the indispensable basics step by step in what experience shows is language that students really understand—then this new book is for you.

It's a method that I taught orally for twenty years in response to the real needs of community college and university students—who aren't going to be literary artists but who are certainly going to have to learn how to write competently, both for the courses they take while they're in college and for their life work as employees, employers, or professional people. If you too are eager to do the most with the talents of each of the young men and women you find in your classroom on the first day of the term, then you'll find that this book really accomplishes what you want a composition textbook to accomplish.

I said that I taught my course in response to the real needs of students, so you gather that it's based not on theory, but on experience. What I've found is that freshmen don't want advice on how to improve their themes; they want to know how to write a theme, from scratch. So I begin with the very first step, and when they can all do that—as they all can—I take them to the second step and then to the third, and on to the point where finally all of them—all—are writing competently.

Another thing I've found is that even the brightest students don't understand very well, if at all, that a theme must have a clear point and that it's the whole business of a theme to support that point in a logical way. But it does no good just to tell students that; you must teach them to do it—which is exactly what this book does.

I say the book does it, because this isn't a reference book for students to refer to while the instructor is left to create the course. It itself is the course and supplies the principles, explanations, examples, assignments, and even the answers to student objections. I've taught foreign languages and found doing so unbelievably easy when compared with teaching English precisely because (besides there being no themes to correct, needless to say) the course was right in front of me in the book. The book took the students methodically from lesson to lesson, each lesson furnished with everything necessary for the students' mastery.

Because I could find no book that did the same for English composition, I wrote this one. In doing so, I transcribed the oral instruction I've been giving my classes for years. As a result, the book addresses the student easily, familiarly, and directly: it is a conversation with the student. For my object hasn't been to sound professional; my object has been to teach.

At the same time the course in this book is highly structured and teaches highly structured writing—which is just what students want and certainly need. Far from restricting students, the tight structure soon frees them to say what they really want to say. Their themes become as individual as their handwriting. And students endowed with gifts of expression find at last a form in which they can put those gifts to meaningful use.

In fact, what will please you most—as it pleases me most—is that on completing the course students will be enthusiastic about their own writing and the good, solid sense it makes when they reread it.

William J. Kerrigan

CONTENTS

WRITING TO THE POINT

Step 1 is very simple. But before we begin with Step 1, I'd like to say something helpful about the method in this book. It *is* a method, a step-by-step method, and that is what makes this book different from others that you may have used. The book itself, as you'll see at once, talks directly and familiarly with you, instead of formally to your instructor; so it is not so much a book as a conversation.

Now what I want to say is that the method taught in this book has proved useful to everyone from grade school students to graduate students in English. (As a matter of fact, one excellent writer, the head of a college English department, told me gratefully that he had learned some things of value from it.) But what you'll really like to hear is that out of the thousands of high school and college students who have studied this method, not one has failed to learn to use it. And after learning it, not one has failed to write themes that, as he himself could see, were quite acceptable—the kind of theme that he had never dreamed he could write.

I suspect that what lies behind this method is my experience with

swimming. Efforts to teach me to swim, beginning back in my grade school days, had time after time proved utter failures. In crowded municipal pools, in small private pools, and in the swimming holes in rural creeks, my friends told me to do this and do that, gave me one piece of advice and then another, held me up as I waved my arms and legs, put water wings on me, demonstrated for me again and again. No use. I couldn't learn to swim a stroke or to keep myself up in the water for one second.

But one day when I was in my twenties and was paddling my hands in the water in the shallow end of a pool—while other people swam—a friend of mine got out of the water and said, "Walk out there ten or fifteen feet and turn and face me on the deck of the pool here. O.K. Now raise your hands above your head, take a deep breath and hold it, close your eyes if you want to, and just lie face down in the water. You absolutely can't sink. Then, when you're out of breath, stand up again."

I followed his directions and to my surprise I didn't sink.

"Now," he said, "when you lie down again in the water, just kick your feet up and down and you'll come right to me at the edge of the pool."

I did as he told me. When my hands met the side of the pool and I stood up again, I realized that after years of vain effort, I had—in less than five minutes—learned how to swim. It was the simplest kind of swimming to be sure; and I need not take you through the steps that followed, in which I moved my arms, lifted my head to breathe, and developed various strokes. Let me say only that today I have an acceptable swimming technique.

When it came to teaching theme writing, then, I imagine I realized that for a method that was going to work for all students, good, fair, and indifferent, what was necessary was a set of simple instructions that any and every student could follow, that would lead—like "lie face down in the water"—to automatic success. The foolproof method that I developed is fully contained in this book. But before turning to that method, I have a few more helpful words to say. First, remember that it guarantees that you will write acceptable themes. And that is because it is automatic: it relies on itself, not on any skill of yours; it does not depend on your having good ideas, a good vocabulary, or good expression. For that reason, it cannot guarantee that the themes you produce will be literature. (To produce literature you would ordinarily need to have done a lot of reading and writing, besides, of course, having been born with unusual gifts.)

But after all, what call will there ever be for you to write literature? In your government class, in your psychology class, in your anthropology class, if your instructor requires you to write a paper, what he will want is a decent, clear, orderly, detailed explanation of something, not a beautiful personal essay. Similarly, in later life, when you have to write a report for your employer or employees, for your customers, or for your colleagues, the people you write for will not expect a masterpiece. But they will want a clear explanation of something that they need to understand. To teach you to do that kind of writing is the modest but useful purpose of this book.

Some of you may write literature later on and if so will find this book a good foundation for it. Meanwhile, if we are all to achieve the modest goal of this book, you will have to do some work—though I must keep assuring you that it will be work you, whoever you are, *can* do. As I have told you, the fundamental secret of swimming was revealed to me by my friend in a flash. But I did not then become a decent swimmer without hours of practice in the pool. We learn to swim by—and *only* by—swimming; we learn to skate by skating; and you—as you don't recall but I'm sure believe—learned to walk by walking. It should not surprise you, then, that we learn to write by writing.

So first of all, you'll have to apply your mind to the instructions that go with each step in this method. You can understand the instructions; they're not as hard as the rules of football, basketball, pinochle, driving a car, or making your own clothes. And you can follow a football game, play cards, drive, or make your own clothes, can't you? But you probably won't understand the instructions without some effort—they're not as simple as "touch your right ear."

Believe me when I tell you, however, that what you *don't* understand in this book you won't need in order to write an acceptable theme. You'll get the main ideas, all right. Sometimes you'll go along, maybe even for several pages, saying, "This stuff is too deep for me. I don't know what it's in here for anyway." Right! That material is here because *some* students will find it helpful for the kind of theme *they* write. But it needn't worry you.

So if you're occasionally baffled by something as you study the six steps, be patient and do not become discouraged. I can see how your first puzzlement may come, for example, in the first chapter, where I compare a certain sentence to a magnet. You may say, "I don't think I really see the point. And especially I don't see whether I'm supposed to be learning something here or not." Go right on and don't worry. The magnet—or whatever else you don't understand—isn't important.

At the same time, don't be timid. If you don't understand something, give it at least a second try before going on to the next thing. You're brighter than you think you are, you know.

Besides understanding as much as you can, you'll have to write themes to show yourself you can apply the rules—and to get practice, of course. Actually, a dozen practice themes of two or three hundred words should be enough to make you a decent writer.

"But," you object (and this will be only the first of your objections), "that's just the point: I can't write a theme." Have no fear. Just follow the instructions, simple step by simple step, and you'll automatically be writing a theme before long. "Just take a deep breath and lie face down in the water."

Finally, I'll make a bargain with you. I can't give you clear directions and at the same time answer all your objections. But I promise to answer your objections later on, when the answers won't get in the way of something else; and I'll also give you the reasons behind each step.

Let's look at one specific objection, though, and a partial answer to it. Particularly if you feel and have been told that you already write well, the method that follows may at first strike you as cramping your style by (a) keeping you from saying what you want to say and (b) forcing you to do very meager, bare, thin, mechanical writing. But you can be sure as you go on that if you're patient, you will find that the very opposite is true. The method we are about to begin will allow you to employ all your talents in a fuller way than you have ever been able to employ them before. Just take a deep breath and lie face down in the water.

I'd like to tell you something now, before we begin Step 1, and ask you to remember it throughout this book. Will you? It is this: the method you are about to follow is not something new. It is simply a description of the *basic* things all writers do today and did yesterday and hundreds of years before that. And I want you to keep in mind that they do them and did them not because they're the right way to do things according to some English teacher, but because they're the main way, the necessary way, of helping *readers* to follow what a writer is saying and to get a clear picture of it.

STEP 1

Write a sentence.

"Well, nothing could be simpler than that," you say. All right, but be sure that it's a *sentence,* because everything depends on that. The following, for example, are *not* sentences: "Why grandpa pretended to be dead"; "My summer on a cattle ranch"; "Working in a gold mine"; "Why we should study anthropology." No, a sentence makes a definite statement—without any why's or where's or if's to depend on. It tells us that somebody (or something) *is* something—or *was* something, or *does* something, or *did* something.

$$\left.\begin{array}{l}\text{Somebody}\\\text{Something}\end{array}\right\} \quad \left\{\begin{array}{l}\text{is or was}\\\text{does or did}\end{array}\right\} \quad \text{something.}$$

For instance, "The child is crying"—can you see that somebody is *doing* something in that set of words? That's what makes it a sentence. Notice that same thing in the following sentences.

Dogs bark.
My father was a plasterer.
Power corrupts.
Two plus three equals five.
Energy equals mass times velocity squared.
Grandpa pretended to be dead.
I learned self-reliance on a cattle ranch.
Last summer I worked in a gold mine.
Every college student's education should include anthropology.

If you still have trouble recognizing a sentence, perhaps your instructor can find out what your difficulty is and help you. For the ability to know what a sentence is, is absolutely necessary, since anything *but* a sentence will no more work as Step 1 than a ping-pong ball will work as a football or a pile of jacks will work as a deck of cards.

But perhaps you'll grasp what I mean when I tell you that *the statement you write for Step 1 is not a title or heading of any kind.* Sometimes when students write their statement for Step 1, they write a sentence, but they show that they think of it as a title by writing it in capital letters—for instance: I WORKED IN A GOLD MINE. No! The sentence in Step 1 is not a title. Get that out of your head. It's going to be a sentence in your theme—a definite, complete statement of a fact or a theory.

So, write a sentence.

Any sentence? Well, theoretically yes, any sentence. But for your purposes here I must be more specific. First, this original sentence that you're writing for Step 1 ought to be short and simple: "High school is different from grade school"; "Cigarette smoking is dangerous to your health"; "Keats was a Romantic poet." As you will see later, if the sentence in Step 1 isn't short and simple, you'll be in trouble when you reach Step 2.

Second, the sentence is to be a statement (called a declarative sentence), not a question or a command. That is, it is not to be a question, like "Why is cigarette smoking dangerous?" or "Was Keats a Romantic poet?" Nor is it to be a command, like "Don't start smoking" or "Practice writing at least one paragraph a day."

Third, be sure your sentence for Step 1 makes only one statement, not two or more. Don't try to use a sentence like "Smoking is dangerous and expensive." That's two statements: one that smoking is dangerous, the other that it's expensive. For Step 1, say that it's dangerous or say that it's expensive, but don't say both.

STEP 1

7

Fourth, let me explain that each new step casts light on the preceding steps (if a step can be said to cast light). So if you ask whether Step 1 can be any sentence that meets the conditions I've given, let me say for now that you will soon be able to tell very well that some sentences will suit your purposes while others will not. For instance, the sentence "My father was a plasterer," given as an example a few sentences back, would prove only fairly useful to you. As I'll say when I discuss Step 2, sentences that tell how something looks (description), what happened (narration), how to make or do something or how something works (process) will not suit your purpose. But let's cross that bridge when we come to it. Meanwhile, we've made Step 1 more specific.

STEP 1

Write a short, simple declarative sentence that makes one statement.

Assignment

Do Step 1 as your first assignment, and the writing part of this lesson is done. Do it right now, and put it in your notebook for future consideration.

Next, since the written work for this lesson is so short and easy, you can spend some time rereading what you've read so far. The first thing to make sure you've gotten out of what you've read is that, just as by following my friend's simple directions I couldn't *not* swim, you, by following my directions, can't *not* write an acceptable theme. You're bound to succeed. Or, if you already write well and think that this work is too simple for you, just be patient and consider the following story.

When I was a young child, an older cousin of mine presented me with a simple bar of iron and told me that I could do lots of tricks with it. Being a bright little boy, however, I was quite skeptical about the powers of an old piece of iron! But in a few minutes I learned that that short, simple iron bar had a magic property I had never heard of and would never have dreamed of. It was magnetized! And I certainly could perform with it tricks I had never imagined possible. Well, in somewhat the same way, the short, simple sentence of Step 1, though seemingly almost powerless, has certain wonderful qualities that, once you've begun to suspect they're there, you could spend years exploring.

All the first half of this chapter, which I've asked you to reread, is actually a preface. But if I had called it a preface, you probably wouldn't have read it; so I smuggled it into this first lesson because I think that knowing you're going to succeed—can't *not* succeed—is the biggest extra help this book can give you. The second thing you should get out of this chapter is all I've said about Step 1 itself. Go over that part thoughtfully, because every word will prove helpful. Reread this whole lesson carefully—now or later—before going on to the next one.

This lesson is quite long, perhaps too long to be digested as a single meal. I have therefore divided it into sections, each of which you can regard as a single lesson. There is no writing assignment until the very end; but you can do reading assignments by rereading each section carefully, doing your best (which is good enough for me) to make sure that you are following what I'm saying. Of course, you may not be interested in following it; but remember that it wasn't intended to entertain you, but to teach you something that you're going to need to know.

Your instructor or a friend will come in handy here if you have questions or objections. But let me anticipate one possible objection from readers who already have had some successful experience in writing: remember that Step 2 is only Step 2; in it we do not begin the theme proper or even get into the first paragraph of the theme itself.

A

Step 2 will ask you to do a kind of thinking you've probably never done before. (Steps 4 and 6 will ask you for still other new kinds of thinking.) But it is a kind of thinking, I've discovered, that everyone can do if he decides to try. Still, it is easier *not* to do it; through laziness, you may try to cheat yourself by juggling Steps 1 and 2 so as to avoid that thinking. Granted, this book has promised you automatic success, but no *automated* success! You can't push a button and have a theme pop out. Lifting weights, you know, will certainly increase your muscular strength—but not if you just leave them in the corner and never lift them!

In the same way, then, the method presented here will be a successful method for you, but only if you *use* the method. And to use it, you will have to pay a reasonable amount of attention, exert yourself to a reasonable amount of understanding, do a reasonable amount of thinking, and perform a reasonable amount of work. So promise yourself that you'll be honest with Step 2.

STEP 2

Write three sentences about the sentence in Step 1.

Step 2 is so briefly worded that it contains a couple of traps, so I'm going to have to reword it in a minute. Meanwhile, let me define "three sentences." "Three sentences" means three short, simple declarative sentences, each making only one statement—just as in Step 1. Mind you, they must be *sentences.* So far, so good. But here is the trick, visible in this completer wording of Step 2.

STEP 2

Write three sentences about the sentence in Step 1 —about the whole of that sentence, not just something in it.

You ought to reread Step 2 a couple of times so that you're familiar with it. Let me clarify its instructions by example.

Suppose my sentence in Step 1—let's label it sentence X—is "Coal is being used less and less." Next, Step 2: I have to write three sentences about that sentence. And let's say that for the first of them I write, "Coal is of two kinds, anthracite and bituminous." Ignore the fact that my sentence may seem to make two statements instead of one. Otherwise, think about it: "Coal is of two kinds, anthracite and bituminous." Read sentence X again: "Coal is being used less and less." And now my sentence 1: "Coal is of two kinds, anthracite and bituminous."

Do you see anything? Do you find anything wrong? Do you understand, with certainty, that I have not really followed the instructions in Step 2? If you see that, you have grasped—believe me—the whole essence of composition. And you are right: "Coal is of two kinds, anthracite and bituminous" is about coal, all right, but it is *not* about the fact that coal is being used less and less. In other words, my sentence is not about the *whole* of sentence X; it is just about some-thing (coal) *in* sentence X.

Now before beginning the next paragraph, please reread the first part of this lesson, from the beginning up to this point.

After you've reread up to this point, it's natural for you to want an example of a series of sentences in which the writer has followed Step 2 correctly. All right, how about this.

> X Coal is being used less and less.
> 1. Coal is being replaced by oil and gas in heating houses.
> 2. Coal-burning locomotives have all been replaced by diesels.
> 3. Industry increasingly turns from coal to other sources of power.

Whatever else you may feel about these three sentences, I think you'll agree that they are truly about the whole of sentence X. They are three reasons, or three pieces of evidence, for sentence X.

Before I try to clinch my point with some more examples of a sentence X followed by faulty sentences 1, 2, and 3, let me say one thing. Examples of right ways and wrong ways to do Step 2 may seem to you to go on and on here, with one just suggesting another, and you may begin to ask, "What's all this leading to? What am I supposed to get out of all this?" The answer is that you have already gotten out of this chapter what you're supposed to get; you have already caught on to Step 2. But it's tricky, so you need practice in it. I'm giving you a lot of practice in it in what follows. All you have to do is read it and know that it's clinching your understanding of Step 2. So let's go on with the examples.

Let's say my sentence X is "Aunt Olga has a bad temper," and let's say my sentence 1 is "Aunt Olga was born in 1914." She was born in 1914? What has that to do with her having a bad temper? Am I attempt-ing to say that babies born in 1914 were unusually likely to grow up having bad tempers? No, my sentence 1 won't work. We'll have to cross it out and start again. How about "She loses her temper at least three times a day"? That sentence may come a little too close to just repeating sentence X, but at least it has something to do with the fact that Aunt Olga has a bad temper; it's not just some random fact (like *born in 1914*) about Aunt Olga that has nothing to do with the fact that she has a bad temper.

But let's take a more difficult example.

> X To be educated, we should study anthropology.
> 1. In anthropology we study the customs of primitive peoples.

STEP 2

13

2. In anthropology we study the social relationships of primitive peoples.
3. In anthropology we study the myths of primitive peoples.

Study this example and see what you think of it. (If, after studying it, you don't understand the discussion of it that follows, don't worry. There's more for you in the material that comes a little later. But try now to concentrate on the example I've just given.) Something is wrong with this example (and I don't mean that the writer should have given anthropology its wider meaning, the study of all peoples, primitive or not; the writer's choice of the restricted meaning is perhaps legitimate, and in any case not what we're quarreling with). Remember that the writer's original assertion—his sentence X—is that to be educated we should study anthropology. That's what his sentence *is;* that's what he *says;* and that—not something else he may have had in the back of his mind—is what his sentences 1, 2, and 3 *must* be about. And please notice that. For in writing themes, you are dealing strictly with what you put down on paper, not with what you have in mind but do not have down on paper.

Passing over any debate about what being educated means—since we can suppose that the writer expects us all to agree pretty much on that—we are still faced with the fact that in sentences 1, 2, and 3 the writer says nothing about a study of customs, social relationships, and myths as being *necessary for education.* It's as if he'd said in sentence X "Oxygen is necessary for life" and then for sentence 1 said "Oxygen has an atomic weight of 15.9994." What has oxygen's having an atomic weight of 15.9994 to do with its being necessary for life?

So it looks as if the writer either forgot what he intended to show about anthropology, or else just put anthropology into any old sentence X—the first one that came into his mind or looked important—and then paid no more attention to sentence X and went on to talk at random about anthropology as a general topic. In other words, he seems to have ignored the very point of Step 2.

What he might have done is this: seeing that his sentence X and his sentences 1, 2, and 3 weren't really connected, he might have studied sentences 1, 2, and 3 to see what they had in common and then produced a new sentence X out of that.

X Anthropology is a study concerned with primitive peoples.
1. It deals with their customs.
2. It deals with their myths.
3. It deals with their social relationships.

You may say, "But what has become of his original subject? You've made a new subject up for him yourself." No. First of all it was he, in his sentences 1, 2, and 3, who completely abandoned his original assertion that anthropology is a necessary part of an education. Second, I did not make up a new subject for him; I got the only subject I could find out of his own sentences 1, 2, and 3.

At this point you may object, "This seems to be more about anthropology than about writing themes!" Be patient. Our imaginary writer's sentences X, 1, 2, and 3 have to be about *something.* He wrote about anthropology, and we have to say a little about it so as to say how he wrote about it. Pretend that *you* had written about it, and you'll see the point of discussing it.

So what else could he—or you—have done to make sentences X, 1, 2, and 3 come out all right? Well, yes, he could have kept his own original assertion—his own sentence X—and figured out a series 1, 2, and 3 that would really fit it. I can only guess what his sentences 1, 2, and 3 would then be: something, perhaps, about learning from primitive beliefs and practices that our way of looking at things is not the only way—which is one of the products of true education, certainly; then something about the fact that beneath all the differences between peoples, human nature in every time and place has proved ultimately the same—another product of education, of course. He might have added the assertion that we do not get enough of these products of education from history and geography. Anyway, he has to do *something* to make sentences 1, 2, and 3 really say something about sentence X.

Personally, I think asserting "To be educated, we should study anthropology" sets up something too hard to prove. Wouldn't it be enough to say "Anthropology is truly educational"? We ought not, in our sentence X, to bite off more than we can chew.

There is still another possibility. The writer may feel that he *was* right in choosing the sentence X and the sentences 1, 2, and 3 that he did—for reasons, however, that I want to delay discussion of. But I'll come back to it.

In this section I want to add something more about sentence X in general. I was saying in the last section that in sentence X we ought not to bite off more than we can chew. This is a reminder of what I told you in the first lesson: that each step casts light on steps that have gone before, and that later on in this book you will be able to tell which sentences will suit your purposes for sentence X and which not. Let's discuss a sample sentence fully. "My father was a plasterer" is only fairly suitable because, as you can see, there are hardly three sentences that you can say about it. True, you could say that a plasterer does this, that, and the other thing, but those things are true of all plasterers, and the fact that your father was a plasterer hardly enters into the matter.

But I would not rule the sentence out. For you can imagine a child's asking you, "What did your father do?" You'd say, "He was a plasterer." But then the child would say, "Oh? What did he *do?*" Then you would go on to say what he, like any plasterer, did. (Often it is useful to think about sentence X as the answer to a question—"What is anthropology?" "Is anthropology educational?" Thinking of it as the answer to a question will probably suggest at once a good series 1, 2, and 3.)

But let's take for another example the sentence "My name is Lloyd Palfy." It's not suitable for a sentence X because there's no more to be said—no series 1, 2, and 3 possible. Oh, you *could* force yourself to say, "Lloyd is from the Welsh *llwyd,* meaning 'gray'; I was named that as a baby not because I was gray, but because Lloyd is my uncle's name. Palfy is from the Welsh *ap-alfy,* meaning 'son of Alfy (Alfred)'; but I'm not really the son of Alfy, for my father's name is Llewellyn, not Alfy. Palfy is a name given to some ancestor whose father *was* Alfy and who passed the name down to us as a permanent surname." But is that natural? When somebody asks you your name and you give it, does it ever occur to you to add an explanation like that? No. Sentences 1, 2, and 3 should follow on sentence X naturally and usefully.

Of course, having written as sentence X "My name is Lloyd Palfy," you might go on, for sentences 1, 2, and 3, to give other facts about yourself: where you live, what you do, and so forth. But if you did that, you would simply be ignoring Step 2. For remember, you wrote "My name is Lloyd Palfy," and according to Step 2 you are stuck with discussing what your name is *and nothing else.* Where you live and what you do have nothing to do with what your name is.

The moral is: be sure you are very careful about your selection of sentence X, because you are stuck with talking *only about what it says*—the *whole* of what it says.

You may unconsciously want to avoid the work that Steps 1 and 2 involve. When you are asked to write a theme—say, about a relative—you may come up with a sentence X like "Uncle Ralph is a wonderful man." That sentence is so broad and vague that it says nothing; all it does is allow the lazy writer to say just about anything about Uncle Ralph in sentences 1, 2, and 3. No, sentence X must be somewhat more particular and definite: "Uncle Ralph is a miser"; "Uncle Ralph is a pinochle addict"; "Uncle Ralph can repair anything from a lawn mower to radar equipment"; "Uncle Ralph is a hypochondriac."

Those sentences really determine the kind of thing you're going to have to say in sentences 1, 2, and 3—as "Uncle Ralph is a wonderful man" does not. So if you're tempted to write "Aunt Jane is unique" as your sentence X, think again! It's not a good sentence X, because it allows you to say almost *anything* about Aunt Jane: she knits beautiful sweaters; she takes in stray dogs; she once won a beauty contest in North Dakota.

Now I told you that Step 2 would involve a kind of thinking you'd probably never done before. You get the point, don't you? Let's see if you do. Some people, having heard all this explanation, when asked to write a series X, 1, 2, and 3 about some teacher they've had, write as sentence X something like "Miss López was my geometry teacher." Now either such a writer understood *nothing* of what I've said—and that's hard to believe—or else he has decided that he is not going to bother with Steps 1 and 2 and is simply going to write not on a sentence, but on a topic—namely, Miss López. Then for sentences 1, 2, and 3 he feels free to say just anything that comes into his head about Miss López: she dressed attractively; she gave low grades; she was also a gym teacher.

Now she did all those things whether she was the writer's geometry teacher or not; they have no connection with sentence X. The only sentences 1, 2, and 3 that I can think of that could be connected to "Miss López was my geometry teacher" would be evidence that she *was* his geometry teacher: the records at Umber Heights High School, the testimony of his classmates, the agreement of Miss López herself. Remember, what the student wrote was that Miss López was his geometry teacher; his sentences 1, 2, and 3, therefore, have to be strictly about that fact *and nothing else.*

You'd better reread the example about Miss López and all I've said about it until it becomes crystal clear.

C

Now in this section we can look at another kind of example.

> X There are three reasons you should write themes on only one side of the paper.
> 1. Since you can get paper for only a fifth of a penny per sheet, you'll look miserly if you use both sides.
> 2. Some teachers (whom it is unwise to offend) will feel it a discourtesy if you use both sides.
> 3. Despite the direction *over,* what is written on the back of a page sometimes gets overlooked.

To that kind of sentence X I have no general objection, for it does serve to organize meaningfully, in a reader's mind, the material that follows—that is, it lets the reader know at the outset what point the material that follows is supposed to add up to. It is, moreover, a form of sentence X that you will sometimes find convenient when you have only a few minutes in which to organize an idea and to get about 150 words down on paper. Notice, for example, that it does make a statement capable of development and that it even provides the helpful clue of what form the reader can expect that development to take (reasons).

True, it is not the best kind of sentence X. Why not? Notice that it *promises* to say something instead of actually saying it. So it would be better if for the same series 1, 2, and 3 we could write a sentence X that would say all that sentences 1, 2, and 3 say, but not in the detail in which they say it. Then we would have something like this.

> X Savings from writing themes on both sides of the paper are not worth the inconveniences.
> 1. The saving of a fifth of a cent a page will make you look miserly.
> 2. The practice is an unwise offense to some teachers.
> 3. Despite the warning *over,* sometimes the writing on the back of a page gets overlooked.

Now, if you'll look at it, the sentence X here does say everything—but in brief. Then sentences 1, 2, and 3 go into detail. But the sentence X that simply promises that the writer will say something remains respectable. You may expect a good professional writer to write a sentence X like "American education and English education are different" and to follow it with a series of sentences about the principal differences, even though he might have contained his whole essay in a sentence X like this: "English education, unlike American education, seeks selectively to provide the nation with leaders educated in depth, and hence trained to think in depth."

There remains to say that, for the purposes of this program, you are not to use a sentence X which (a) is descriptive (tells how something looks), (b) is narrative (tells what happened), or (c) introduces a process (tells either how to make or do something or how something works). True, papers on such subjects are perfectly good in themselves. You will have occasions in life, certainly, to write such papers. (This very book is nothing but a long process paper.) But they are—fortunately for all of us—too easy. They usually involve only a space relationship ("to the left," "above," "further along") or a time relationship ("first," "next," "then"), with perhaps some cause-and-effect relationship involved ("This provides a contrasting background"; "This causes the steam to condense"). Thus they do not present the kind of problem that the program in this book is designed to train you to solve—the kind of problem in writing that you are sure to meet, both in school and later in your business or professional life.

Problems in description, narration, and process writing—though we'll say something about them later—you can solve by yourself. (Extensive professional training in such matters is, of course, provided by courses in creative writing and technical writing.) This book is fundamentally concerned with problems in the relationships of ideas—problems that are part of your education as well as part of learning to write. Such problems are new to you, and they are what you must have practice in solving.

Thus we must rule out here any sentence X like "In June the Iowa countryside has a parklike beauty"; "Making root beer is simple"; or "A diesel engine is easy to understand." We must rule out, too, "My father was a plasterer" if what follows is going to tell the story (narration) of how he became a plasterer.

But you remember that early in this lesson I said that there was still another possibility—which I promised to discuss—open to the writer who told us that anthropology is a necessary part of education and then simply went on to tell us what is taught in anthropology, with no further hint of why anthropology is a necessary part of education. That additional possibility is this: the writer may argue, "Oh yes, these points are connected with anthropology as a necessary part of education; *I intend to show that connection later on.*"

The writer's argument is intelligent. He is not aware at this point, however, that the purpose of sentences 1, 2, and 3, as we will see more clearly later, is to give the reader an *immediate* clue to what he is supposed to be looking for. But because the writer's argument is a natural one, we'll have to reword Step 2 again, inserting the words *clearly and directly.*

STEP 2

Write three sentences about the sentence in Step 1 —clearly and directly about the whole of that sentence, not just something in it.

You see, the writer's sentences 1, 2, and 3 may eventually prove to be connected with his sentence X. But we don't know. And that's just the point. We ought to know, clearly and at once. That's why we have to put into Step 2 the words *clearly and directly.*

Admittedly, to conclude, you are left with the task of inventing those three sentences. How do you go about it? A good way to go about it is to decide what questions, or what kind of question, a reader would naturally ask after you announce your sentence X. Then let sentences 1, 2, and 3 provide explanations or answers. (If you *can't* think of any questions a reader might ask, then you probably have as dead-end a sentence X as "My name is William Jones.")

In summary, what should you have gotten out of this long lesson? First, that anyone of normal—even low-normal—intelligence can grasp and apply Step 2. (I would expect the brilliant person to grasp and apply it brilliantly.) So intelligence is not what we are worried about. Honesty and diligence are far more important here, as in the whole of life. Have I honestly avoided descriptive, narrative, and process subjects in my sentence X? Have I honestly taken the trouble to think up a sentence X about the whole of which I can write a series 1, 2, and 3? Are my sentences 1, 2, and 3—honestly—connected in a clear and direct way with my sentence X?

Before you begin your next assignment, you may as well know that Step 2 isn't really limited to three sentences. It could be four or five or any greater number. But for the time being, three will be enough. Not two (or one)—that is not enough. "Three" in Step 2 means three or more. But unless you personally want to have more, three will be enough for the exercises in this book.

Assignment

Make up as many as a dozen sets of sentences X, 1, 2, and 3. Do each set in the following form.

> X Power corrupts.
> 1. It corrupts the powerful.
> 2. It corrupts the powerless.
> 3. It corrupts every relationship between the two.

You'll find that doing this takes work. It will especially take work—highly profitable work—if you do not restrict yourself to the simplest subjects (cars, sports), but try a few subjects like government, science, literature, or business. In any case, take the assignment seriously.

I need to introduce Step 3 with a serious warning: the theme you will write as the assignment at the end of this chapter will seem to you about as poor a thing as you have ever written. Were it not for the warning I am giving you here, you might say, "Well, if this is his idea of a theme, there's no use going on with his method. 'By their fruits you shall know them,' and look at the miserable apples his tree has produced. No, I'm going back to my own way of writing themes; they may have been only fair, or even poor, but at least they were better than this truck I've just written."

Be patient. First, the theme you will write at the end of this lesson may seem to you really miserable. But let me tell you that though you won't be able to see it right away, what you write will have five qualities of a decent theme. I won't tell you what they are now; you'll find out later. This theme of yours, I agree, will *lack* other necessary qualities, and I'll be glad that you feel that lack (without, probably, being able to put your finger on it, name it, or describe it). For the last three steps—especially Step 4—are designed to take care of that lack.

Thus feeling strongly, if not clearly, the need for those steps, you will be able to take them quite seriously when you come to them.

Second, I'll tell you a story. I learned calligraphy (which you might call printing by hand) from one of the finest calligraphers in the country, a man regarded by many people as the foremost authority on the forms of the letters of our alphabet. Can you imagine how he had me spend the first three months under his instruction? He had me draw lines about one and a half inches long, one after another, line after line, with a reed on old newspapers. First it was vertical lines; then he added horizontal lines; next lines slanting down to the right; then lines slanting down to the left; and finally half circles. This I did, hour after hour, day after day, month after month.

Now I could point out a number of things about that instruction. For instance, it was not what many people call interesting. If I had come to the expert expecting him to "make it interesting," he would have had no time for me, because he had better things to do—but particularly because if I could not myself get interested in my own progress in drawing those simple lines well, then any other "interest" would have been beside the point.

But what I especially want to point out is that the instruction served a twofold purpose, as I saw later. First, of course, it was necessary training to be undergone before I approached the production of actual letters. But second, it was a test, a test of my docility. *Docility* means "teachableness" and is simply the quality of being willing to follow simple instructions and to have confidence in the instructor, who has been through all the learning—and perhaps much teaching—before and just might know what he's doing. If I had not proved my docility, my instructor—who, as I said, had better things to do—would not have wasted a minute on me. Fortunately, I turned out not to be one of those beginners who, at the very beginning, "know" that the instructor is wrong.

Today I, whose talent in art is practically nil, can produce writing (what you would call printing) that the ordinary person marvels at as beautiful. I know myself that my work is decent but certainly not excellent, and for that reason I have not identified my instructor by name—though surely it was a triumph for him to teach someone who has no speck of natural ability to produce work that the ordinary public thinks beautiful.

So, with the final moral from my story—that similarly you, even without any talent, by patiently, docilely, and seriously following a step-by-step method, can produce a good theme—we can ascend Step 3.

STEP 3

Write four or five sentences about each of the three sentences in Step 2.

There are five comments of various kinds that need to be made about Step 3. First, one of the two necessary things in Step 3 is that the sentences you write must be *at least* four or five in number. Some people, in fact, would say that ten would be a better minimum, and I would agree in theory. But four or five will be enough for our purposes. Remember, however, that while fewer than four or five will be totally unacceptable, more than four or five will be very good indeed. Don't worry that I seem to waste time in dwelling on this simple matter; just be sure that *you* always have at least four or five—no fewer!—sentences after each of the three in Step 2.

Second, the first four or five sentences are to be about the whole of the *first* sentence in Step 2, the second four or five about the whole of the *second* sentence in Step 2, and the third four or five about the whole of the *third* sentence in Step 2. There is no need to spend much time on the meaning of "the whole of" here, for that was covered at length in the lesson on Step 2. You understand, of course, that the sentences in Step 3 bear the same relationship to the sentences in Step 2 as those in Step 2 bore to sentence X in Step 1. So do not grow careless here; remember that the directions "clearly and directly about the whole of" remain all-important.

Third, have no fear—you will be happy to learn that Step 4 is not going to be "Now write ten or eleven sentences about each of those five"! The branching out—from one to three to twelve or fifteen—is now at an end. But notice this: sentence X and the three sentences in Step 2 had to be short and simple statements because you now have to write additional sentences about the whole of the statements that each of them made. Now when you come to these four or five additional sentences and realize that you are not going to have to write more about each of them, you see that they don't need to be short and simple. Nor should they all be! You will have long sentences and short sentences, simple sentences and complex sentences, sentences making just one statement, others making several.

Fourth, though, as just indicated, you are to take care not to have the sentences in Step 3 a series of short baby sentences, you are *not* at this point to worry at all about the *quality* of these sentences. That is a very special matter to be taken up in another step. Don't worry at all about whether these sentences are "good"; just take care that there are at least four or five of them and that some of them, at least, are of pretty good length. (I can't give you an exact number of words; just write some of the longer sentences you would normally write.)

Fifth, I am giving you, last of all, the way I want you to arrange your paper on your page. First, just as you did in the preceding assignment, put down sentence X (Step 1), labeling it *X*. Directly underneath it put down sentences 1, 2, and 3 in a column, labeling them *1, 2,* and *3*. Then draw a broken line across the page under what you've just done.

Next, under the broken line, indent as you do when you start a new paragraph and *copy down* sentence X, labeling it *X*. Under this, indent in the same way and *copy down* your sentence 1 from Step 2, labeling it *1*. Then, without further indentation and without (this is highly

STEP 3

25

important) any further numbers or letters, write the four or five or more sentences that go with sentence 1 (Step 3). Then indent, copy down sentence 2, and proceed as with sentence 1; and finally, in the same way, indent and copy down sentence 3 and its four or five sentences.

This form is shown in the following example. The *content* of the example, as you'll see at once, is poor, for the writer has chosen too simple a subject and has made his four or five sentences short, simple, and repetitious in form. But because his theme *is* so simple, it gives you a good example of the correct physical form—the way your theme is to look on the page. *You are to use this form throughout this program. Every theme assigned is to look this way.*

X I dislike winter.
1. I dislike the winter cold.
2. I dislike having to wear the heavy winter clothing that cold weather requires.
3. I dislike the colds that, despite heavy clothing, I always get in the winter.

———————————————————————————

X I dislike winter.
1. I dislike the winter cold. It makes me shiver. It chaps my lips. It gives me chilblains. It can even freeze my ears.
2. I dislike having to wear the heavy winter clothing that cold weather requires. I have to wear earmuffs. I have to wear galoshes. I have to wear a heavy coat. I have to wear long underwear.
3. I dislike the colds that, despite heavy clothing, I always get in the winter. They stop up my nose. They give me a cough. They give me a fever. They make me miss school.

Each of your papers from now on is to be arranged just like the preceding example. For though I dislike red tape just as much as you do, there are good reasons for using this arrangement. Just one simple reason is that it allows your teacher or a friend helping you, but more important, *you yourself,* to see at a glance exactly what you are doing. It would take a lot of time to discuss some of the other, more complicated reasons, and I should get on to the point that, while you are imitating the form of the example I've given, you will surely not want to imitate its Dick-and-Jane style. You cannot yet, perhaps, handle a subject more difficult than "I dislike winter," but your sentences can be more grown up than those your little brother is reading in his primer.

Yet despite the see-Dick-run style, I repeat that the theme itself has five qualities to be found in even the best of themes. They are: (1) a theme sentence that announces its point at once; (2) a topic sentence for each paragraph that is clearly and directly related to the theme sentence; (3) paragraphs that are clearly and directly related to their topic sentences and are well developed; (4) specific examples; and (5) the use of a transitional phrase in the second and third topic sentences to link them to the paragraphs preceding them.

Assignment

Choose your own subject and write a paper following Steps 1, 2, and 3 (just as the theme above does). Arrange it on the page in the same way as the theme above. Do *not* worry if it doesn't seem to be a "good" theme.

Finally, *save* every theme you write until you have finished this course. Sometimes we'll look at your old themes again.

STEP

Do you think of yourself as a poor student? Perhaps you are just still *behind* others rather than really poorer than they. In any case, what you meet here is a long, long chapter. Moreover, while you will find most of the individual parts clear, there are so many of them that as you read along, you may begin to feel confused. Don't worry. Read the whole chapter anyway. And by all means do the several assignments in it as well as you can. Then, when you reach the Summary at the end, don't feel responsible for understanding and remembering the rest of the chapter. All the extra things that aren't in the Summary will be fine for other students, but you'll be able to write your themes—good themes—without them.

When you reach that Summary, though, study it well, and in the assignment that follows it do your level best to follow the instructions in it. You may not do well on that assignment; many people do not. But don't be discouraged. You'll find yourself doing better—and will be pleased with yourself for doing better—as you move along.

Anyway, Step 4—for everybody—is the place where the battle be-

gins. For although this step is the most important of all, and although any beginning writer *can* without difficulty both understand the instructions given and apply them, in nine cases out of ten he simply *won't.*

Why? I have no idea. If I could discover why, then I could proceed without difficulty. But as things stand, I—we—must proceed *with* difficulty. For, of course, beginning writers do eventually put Step 4 into practice; there would be no reason for this book if they didn't. But for some reason, to get them to do so is like trying to open a rusty lock.

What is to be done? First, to oil the lock, I'm going to give you some intermediate exercises. Second, as I have always done in my classes, I'll criticize your first themes extensively. (Of course, I haven't developed ESP sufficiently to be able to do that at long distance! So if you're not using this book as a textbook in class, if you have no instructor to criticize your papers for you, you must criticize them yourself—under my direction. You can do it if in doing it you use all the seriousness, earnestness, and capacity for hard work that are in you.

For, like so many valuable things in life, it doesn't require any particular amount of intelligence—only serious hard work.) Third, I'll divide this chapter into sections, each with an assignment at the end, so that you can consider each section a lesson by itself. Fourth, in this chapter I'll call for more than one theme from you.

But cheer up! You'll master Step 4 in the end. Moreover, you yourself will be pleased with your last paper or two, pleased with yourself for having produced something sound and substantial. Besides, the material you are about to face is not exactly dull; since it calls on you, as I said earlier, to do a kind of thinking you've never done before (but that you *can* do), it has the attractiveness of any new accomplishment.

STEP 4

Make the material in the four or five sentences in Step 3 as specific and concrete as possible.

I think "specific," "concrete," and "as possible" need an explanation.

A

What do you mean by *specific?* We might get at the answer by asking what the opposite of *specific* is. Many people will say *vague.* No, not exactly; the opposite of *vague* is *definite* (and I do not find the followers of my method have any trouble with, or need special training in, being definite). *Specific* here means "special kind of" or "particular." And I think we can all agree that its opposite is *general.*

But there is no exact dividing line between the general and the specific. A word, for example, is usually more general than some words but more specific than others. An example will make this quite clear and will also demonstrate clearly what we mean by *specific* and *general.* Briefly, the specific is a *particular kind* of the general. Thus *a drink* is more general than *tea* (a kind of drink), which is thus more specific than *a drink; oolong* (a particular kind of tea) is more specific still.

Take the word *flower,* for instance. Considered by itself, it's fairly general, yet fairly specific. It's fairly general because we can think of words that are more specific than *flower*—words, that is, that name one or another particular kind of flower. Give me an example of a particular kind of flower. "Rose"? All right, *rose.* Of this pair—*flower, rose*—then, we say that *flower* is the more general and *rose* the more specific. Simple, isn't it? And now that you've seen the example, reread from *A* above down to this point.

Now that you've reread, let's carry the same example further. *Rose* is more specific than *flower;* but what is more specific than *rose?* (Our answer will be a *particular kind* of rose.) How about *moss rose?* Or *American Beauty rose?* Or, if you don't know varieties of rose (and only a fool would expect you to put down on your paper what you don't know), why not just *red rose?*

Now for another example—one that will appeal to many readers—take the word *car.* What's more specific? You can name a make of car. More specific still? The makers of cars give their products a variety of fanciful names with which you are probably familiar; if you're not familiar with them, you can name a year, or a color, or both.

So with *book. Mathematics book* is more specific; *algebra book* more specific still; and *Wicks and Armstrong, Fifth Edition,* about as specific as you can get unless you get down to one particular printing of that book.

Now mind you, this is not just a more or less interesting study of words, but a matter that you'll be using in all your themes from now on. For the rule in Step 4 says that the material in Step 3 is to be *as specific as possible;* and that means that you cannot use *flower* in one of those sentences if it's possible to use *moss rose.* That may shock you! But let me ask at once at least this: do you have to be a genius to say *peppermint ice cream* instead of *food,* or *homemade root beer* instead of *cold drink,* or *dandelions* instead of *weeds?* Can only the talented do that? Or can't it be done by anyone who can order his favorite flavor ice cream, make his own root beer, or weed the front lawn? Yes, any normal person can do it—*if he will.*

Now Step 4 adds the words *if possible.* Later on we'll have to examine this *if possible* at length. Meanwhile, let me anticipate an objection by saying that of course, sometimes you must use the more general word. If you're saying "She loves all flowers," you would defeat your purpose if you changed *flowers* to *African violets.* For "She loves all African violets" is simply not what you meant to say. (Note, though, that if it is not contrary to your purposes, you might *add* fairly specific names of flowers by way of *example.* But more on examples later.)

To finish our study of the general and specific, let's go back to the word *flower* and move this time in the direction of the more general. What is more general than *flower?* I think you will say *plant.* And that's almost as general as you can get, because *greenery, shrubbery,* and *foliage* are not more general than *plant;* they just mean "collections of plants." To get to the more general we have to skip over botanists' distinctions between green plants and, say, fungi, and go to *organism* or *living thing.* Most general of all is *thing* (and it's astonishing how many students will use *thing,* the most general word possible except *being* itself, in an assignment in which they have been instructed to use words that are as specific as possible).

For *car,* a more general term would be *automated land conveyance,* then *automated conveyance* (which would include hydrofoils, dirigibles, and submarines as well), then finally *conveyance* (and, of course, *thing*).

This moving back and forth between the general and the specific is another kind of thinking that you've never been called on to do; being new, it will be a little awkward at first, but it's as necessary for you as learning to separate an egg is for a person first learning to cook. And from now on in your *reading,* both of articles and of stories, you must begin to notice other writers' use of specific words.

Assignment

Take each of the following words and write below it a more specific word, and below that, if possible, a word more specific still. Then above it write a more general word, and above it, if possible, a word more general still. Thus for the word *man* you might list the following.

> living thing
> animal
> *man*
> soldier
> Corporal Charles T. Schwartz

Here are the words you are to practice with.

(1) vegetable, (2) song, (3) student, (4) pen, (5) soda pop, (6) soldier, (7) employment.

You'll find some of these easy and some hard to do. Finally, choose three words of your own and do the same thing.

B

The rule in Step 4 demands also that the material in the four or five sentences of Step 3 be as *concrete* as possible. What is *concrete?* Of course, one meaning is "cement," a mixture of gravel, sand, and powdered rock, but that can hardly be the meaning here. Let's first define *concrete* by stating its opposite—*abstract*—and say that concrete things are things properly speaking, while abstract things are thoughts about things. This will be clear in the following examples.

Boy, chair, pencil, paper, and *room* are all concrete. The test is this: can I see it, rap on it to see what sound results, smell it, taste it, or feel it to see whether it is rough or smooth, hard or soft, hot or cold? Can I paint it a different color, weigh it on a scale, measure it with a ruler, trip over it or run against it, lift it or drop it, move it to the right or the left? If I can do all or some or even one of those things, it is concrete. So *boy, chair, pencil, paper,* and *room* are all concrete.

In contrast, *freedom, justice, bravery, beauty,* and *cooperation* are all abstract. And the test is the same. Can I paint freedom a different color? Feel justice to see whether it is hot or cold? Trip over bravery? Rap on beauty to see whether I get a sharp knock or a dull thud? Smell or taste cooperation? No. In fact, you find those questions pointless or meaningless. Therefore, such words are all abstract.

Of course, any of those abstract words can be used not in its abstract sense, but to name a concrete person or thing. Thus *beauty* can be used to designate not the *quality* of pleasing the observer, but the person or thing that pleases, so that we speak of a woman or a girl as "a beauty," or of a fishing pole, a tennis champion's backhand swing, or a successful pass to left end as "a beauty." A judge on the Supreme Court is called a justice, and Shakespeare by "bravery" sometimes means fine clothes. You yourself, of course, know whether you are using a word abstractly or concretely; but it is not a waste of time to dwell here on an idea that may be quite new to you.

Finally, you will notice that unlike the difference between what is general and what is specific, which is likely to be *relative*—a question of more or less (*jacket* is more specific than *article of clothing* but less specific than *ski jacket*)—the difference between what is abstract and what is concrete is *absolute.* A word is either abstract or it is concrete; there is no question of more or less. The abstract never shades into the concrete; there is a definite, clear-cut difference between them. As we have seen, sometimes in practice a word may be either abstract or concrete, depending on the way it is used. For instance, *music*—if it means the whole art of music, it is abstract; if it refers to singing or playing that you can hear or to a sheet of music that you can see, it is concrete. But it is never half one and half the other.

The next two paragraphs may or may not interest you. They are for students who have a special interest in writing; it would be all right for those of you who don't to skip down to "Back to our real business," on this same page.

At this point some of you may object that the only examples I have given are names of persons and things. "What about verbs—words like *come, go,* and *eat?*" they ask. Well, the answer is that those words may be a matter of concern to you if you advance to considerations not of composition but of style (expression). Let's talk about that here. In this program you will not be required to use only specific verbs (*totter* or *stride* instead of *walk,* or *walk* or *ride* instead of *go*) or only concrete verbs (verbs designating an action you can observe rather than a relationship—*clutch, strike,* or *cheer* rather than *own, hate,* or *admire*). But it won't hurt you to be aware that some verbs are specific or concrete, and others aren't. So too with adjectives: "a *good* book" versus "a *green* book"—*green* you can see (concrete), whereas *good* you cannot. And so with adverbs: *loudly* is concrete, whereas *usually* is likely to be abstract.

By the way, you may have noticed that in this book I tend to use a lot of abstract and general verbs like *is, has,* and *does.* While there is a reason for that, let me emphasize that you are not to use this book as a model—something to imitate—in any way. It will be better for you to imitate the work of most other professional writers, who—also for very good reasons—tend to use varied, specific, even concrete verbs. Yet let me also point out that you shouldn't overdo it: using all colorful, attention-stimulating verbs in a memorandum on why your firm ought to buy a particular kind of padlock would be as much out of place as wearing your best clothes on a camping trip.

Back to our real business, which is that, in the four or five sentences of Step 3, you are to be as concrete as possible. It's important to remember that, though there is a distinct division between the abstract and the concrete, for at least most abstract words there are some concrete things that we can associate with them. Take the abstraction *bravery,* for instance. What persons and things can you associate with it? A soldier, perhaps; a medal; even a short account of a person performing a brave act—Frank Palko dashes into a burning house, finds little Mary Parcelli cowering under a dining-room table, grabs her up and staggers with her to safety. The abstraction *beauty?* A woman; the peaceful and joyous face of an aged minister; a violet; Schubert's *Serenade.*

For your assignment I am going to ask you to take a certain number of abstractions and write down a concrete person or thing that you associate with each . In putting down the concrete person or thing you needn't use just one word; for instance, for *patience* you might put down "a mother feeding her child pureed carrots"; or you might even tell a one-or-two-sentence story, like the one about the daring rescue I just recounted.

But before you begin I want to repeat one thing that is often confused. *Abstract* is not the same as *general,* and *concrete* is not the same as *specific.* For instance, *virtue* is abstract and also quite general; *honesty* (a particular virtue) is more specific, but it is still abstract. *Mailman* is fairly specific and is also concrete; *human being* is far more general, but it is still concrete (after all, we can see a human being, weigh him, and—if he lets us—stand him on his head). If you were given the abstraction *kindness,* you could not give *mercy* as a concrete accompaniment. Mercy is one sort of kindness, all right—an example of it, one might say—but it's still abstract, isn't it? Test it—can you measure its length? Weigh it? Stand it on its head?

Assignment

Here are your abstractions; write down a concrete person or thing you can associate with each.

(1) transportation, (2) confusion, (3) cowardice, (4) art, (5) impatience, (6) ugliness, (7) aviation, (8) orderliness, (9) promptness, (10) success, (11) speed, (12) industriousness.

Next, can you go the other way? Can you take a concrete thing and associate it with an abstraction? (There isn't always just one right answer; you might associate a racing car with *speed, beauty, success, excitement, sport, wealth,* or even perhaps *transportation.*) Can you do it? It can be fun if you'll give yourself to it seriously.

Try, anyway, to associate an abstraction (keep in mind what that is) with each of the following persons and things.

(1) a police officer, (2) a fire extinguisher, (3) a poem, (4) a whip, (5) a flag, (6) a truck, (7) a mother, (8) schoolbooks, (9) a prayer book, (10) vitamin capsules, (11) a school bell, (12) a skeleton.

Finally, choose three abstractions of your own and give each a concrete accompaniment; then choose three concrete persons or things and give each an abstract accompaniment.

C

No, we are not done yet. To be complete, we must give Step 4 a longer wording. We must also explain what we have added to it, and we must have exercises on what we have added.

STEP 4

Make the material in the four or five sentences in Step 3 as concrete and specific as possible. Go into detail. Use examples. Don't ask, "What will I say next?" Say some more about what you have just said. Your goal is to say a lot about a little, not a little about a lot.

Though you may not see any connection between most of the new directions in Step 4 and the shorter version we saw earlier, take my word for it that they add up roughly to the same thing as the original Step 4; the new directions are just specific ways of solving the same problem. But let's examine them one by one: first, "Go into detail."

I taught for some years from a composition book, now long out of print, in which the author asserted that three-fourths of all good writing consists of details, and lots of them, and that the other fourth doesn't matter. Think about it; it's a bold assertion. I'm sure most of us think that the other fourth (which is structure—covered by Steps 1, 2, and 3—and connectedness—covered by Steps 5 and 6) certainly does matter. And I'm sure the author I speak of would have agreed that they do matter, because they're necessary ways of letting the reader follow what you are saying, of keeping him from getting confused. But to emphasize dramatically that without details, writing just can't be called writing, he was willing to go so far as to say that details are the only things that matter.

That author might also have had in mind this: if you wrote a report on the lack of some safety provision in a tin mine and put in it all the details necessary for a full understanding of the point, but didn't put them in a clear order and didn't connect them clearly, an editor who didn't know anything about safety provisions in tin mines could still put your report in good order, with proper connections. But if, on the other hand, you wrote a report without sufficient details, then no matter how good the order and how clear the connections, the editor could do nothing. He couldn't, at his desk, supply the details you were supposed to bring back from the tin mine.

So impress this on your mind: three-fourths of all good writing consists of details, and lots of them; the other fourth doesn't matter. But what are *details?* You already know one use of the term. Suppose you went into a police station and reported that you had just been held up and had lost your wallet or purse. That would be your sentence X (or sentence 1, 2, or 3). The officer at the desk would say "Give me the details," and it would be clear to you that you were to tell him your name and address, where and when the holdup took place, what the holdup man looked like, how he talked, how he was armed, how he left the scene, whether there was a car involved, whether there seemed to be other people with him, and a description of your wallet or purse and its contents, including how much money it contained.

The officer at the desk might ask you for other details, such as where you had been just before the holdup, even where you had been lately, where you were going, whether it was usual for you to be walking where the holdup occurred; and he might or might not explain how such details were relevant. (Note, by the way, that *relevant* means "connected" or "related," and that it begins with *rel-*, just as *related* does.) The officer would not question you on such details as your mother's maiden name, your favorite breakfast food, the color of your pet cat, or your ability to type; those details would be *irrelevant* (not related) to the case: they would be about you, but not about the fact that you were held up.

Now suppose you're writing a theme, and your sentence 1 is "Mail service in the United States has become somewhat faster lately." Now, you can't just add "The Post Office is trying to pick up the mail and ship it in a better way" and then go on to repeat weakly your sentence 1—"This makes the delivery faster. Mail used to be rather slow sometimes, but now it is moving with greater speed. This is an improvement that everyone appreciates. This shows progress on the part of the Post Office."

No, the question is, *How* is the Post Office picking up mail now? And, perhaps, what was the old way? What about the one-star and two-star pickup boxes? What are the new hours of collection, and how do they make mail move faster? How fast is faster? When must I mail my letter so that by tomorrow it will reach an addressee 150 miles away? How is airmail now handled? If sent airmail, will my letter go from coast to coast in two days? If you are writing out of your head and don't know the answers to most of those questions, you obviously should have chosen a subject that you *do* know details about. Or, if you don't know enough details but do have time enough to find them, you'll have to look for them.

Understand that if you say that mail service is faster, or make any other assertion, the reader takes it for granted that you know some *facts,* or have had some experiences, that lead you to make that assertion. After all, your idea didn't just come down out of the sky. And the reader wants to know what those facts or experiences are. *Facts* are the valuable part of your paper—contrary to what you may have believed up till this time. Your *ideas*—which you express in sentences X, 1, 2, and 3—are there only to give point, meaning, and direction to your facts—to show what you think those facts add up to.

Let's take another example. Let's say I assert that my grandfather is neat; I then go on to indicate that he is neat in his person, in his habits, and in his work. That sounds like a set of sentences X, 1, 2, and 3, because I haven't gotten down to any real details yet. Up to that point, here is how the reader is unconsciously reacting: "After all, what is *neat?* I know what *neat* means, of course, but this writer's judgment about neatness and my judgment of it may be different. So what he says isn't meaningless, but it isn't clear yet in my mind what he has in *his* mind when he calls his grandfather neat. Furthermore, though I don't think he's wrong, or lying, I have no way of knowing whether *I'd* call his grandfather neat or not."

The reader doesn't know my grandfather—I do; and I have observed several things about him that have led me to assert that he is neat. If I tell the reader those several things, he will see clearly what I mean and will probably agree with my judgment. In other words, what the reader really wants to know are those several things I've observed about my grandfather that have led me to say he's neat.

So this is the place—and the reason—for details. First, under personal neatness, I should tell how on rising my grandfather shaves; checks to see that his moustache is properly trimmed; vigorously brushes his teeth, his tongue, and his partial plate; and gargles with (name the brand). He then takes a shower, including a shampoo, and finally puts on deodorant (I'd name the brand) and shaving lotion (brand?) and combs his hair. Then he steps into clean clothes and goes downstairs for breakfast.

Next, I'd go into orderliness in Grandfather's personal life: his bed immediately made, his coats and slacks always hung up, his detective novels in neat rows in the bookcases. Then his work habits: as a cabinetmaker he keeps his shop frequently swept; his saws clean, sharpened, and hung up in order; his chisels placed in the proper drawers. And his cabinetwork itself is always flawless.

Of course, I have just begun to give details on each point. But already I hear someone saying, "But that takes so long, and it takes up so much space! What's the point of all that?" Of course it's long. How else do you think you're going to get your four or five—or ten—sentences for Step 3? You're not, I hope, going to just say feebly over again, in slightly different words, what you've already said—"Yes, he's neat, all right. He's even neater than my mother, and that's saying a lot. In fact, he's about the neatest man I ever met. I wish I were that neat. Everyone should be neat."

With that kind of performance—refusal to go into detail, which leaves wholly unanswered the question why you say your grandfather is neat—you're going to end up being the sort of person who in ten minutes covers half or three-quarters of a sheet, then snaps shut his notebook and announces: "I can't think of anything else to say." We must answer such a person with the point of the end of Step 4: it's not a question of thinking of anything else to say; it's a question of saying some more about what you've just said by going into detail.

As for the other question—"What's the point of all this?"—the point is that now the reader can say, "Yes, I see what he means by *neat*. And yes, I'd agree; I'd call his grandfather neat too." He can say it because in my theme I've made myself clear and convincing in the only way anybody *can* make himself clear and convincing—that is, by going into detail.

Of course, what may be in the back of your mind is this: "Nobody cares whether my grandfather is neat. Who's interested in whether he brushes his partial plate vigorously or not?" That's a very important point, one that I'll take up at length later. Meanwhile, without saying I agree or disagree, let me give you two reassurances. First, some of the most absorbing novels in the world, novels that have entertained generations of readers, are made up in part of information just as simple as the information I have just given about my grandfather. Second, you are just practicing now. We are not going to print your theme in the school newspaper. A concert pianist doesn't invite people to come to listen to him practice scales—but he couldn't stay on the concert stage without the practice. So in doing these exercises you are not attempting to create something important. You are practicing on simple things so that when the time comes you'll be able to do well whatever important things you're called on to do.

Finally, note that details take their place in Step 4 because, by their very nature, they are likely to be concrete and specific—more so, at least, than the general statement ("My grandfather is neat") that they are used to explain.

Assignment

Write five to ten (or more) sentences on the sentence "I'd hate to have you see my top bureau drawer." You will doubtless have to use your imagination here—in fact, your top bureau drawer, like mine, may contain only a neatly folded pair of pajamas. In any case, by doing the assignment you will find for yourself what we mean by *details* and surprise yourself with your ability to use them.

Another definition of *detail* is "short example." Now the *details* of a rotary gasoline engine are the fuel-and-air intake opening and area, the compression area, the ignition and explosion area, and the exhaust outlet and area, as well as the curved triangular rotor that is moved by the explosion and the oval chamber that contains the rotor and all the areas. Obviously, these details are the *parts* of the engine, not examples of it. Yet some details might be called examples: Grandfather's using deodorant and keeping his saws hung up may be thought of as *examples* of his neatness.

We often speak of details as examples because whenever we can't give all the details or don't know all the details, we give just a few—in other words, we give examples (meaning "samples") of the details. Thus, for instance, the details I give about Grandfather's neatness are enough, but they're not all I could give. I could tell how he opens letters, how he files his nails, how he folds his money, how he always leaves his pencils sharpened, and so on, indefinitely. The details I do give are examples, or samples of his neatness.

Let me give you a special warning, however: in giving examples of this kind, always give a generous number; don't stop with one or even two. If hard work and honesty are the virtues required for Steps 2 and 3, then hard work and generosity are the virtues required for Step 4—hard work because you cannot allow laziness to keep you from thinking up several examples, and generosity because you cannot allow stinginess to hold you to a bare minimum, like the miser who gives the boy who has swept his walk only a nickel.

Allow me to spend some time on this point, because I suspect that it is more basic than mere rules. You have to be generous in writing, as in life. You have to cast aside your defenses and give yourself to a writing task wholeheartedly. I know that many people refuse to give themselves wholeheartedly to anything. And having given little, they will receive little. Their refusal to give themselves is a kind of selfishness, and few things are more self-defeating than selfishness; because obviously, the selfish person limits himself to himself and never gets beyond himself. Think it over. Strangely but truly, we are never the worse off for being generous. Give yourself wholeheartedly to my writing method, and be particularly generous with examples.

When some writers of composition textbooks speak of examples, they seem to have in mind a single long example. We'll consider them now. I've specified examples in boldface in Step 4 because they are extremely useful, extremely important. They're as important to a writer as a slide rule to an engineer, a drill to a dentist, a large knife to a chef. As a matter of fact, if you took a book (such as is often used in freshman college English) of well-written essays and went from paragraph to paragraph, keeping count, you'd probably find that in many paragraphs—perhaps over half—the second sentence (or sometimes the first) contains the connective *for example,* either understood or more often expressed, either in the words *for example* or in some equivalent like *for instance.*

An example is a wonderful way to make something clear and real and convincing. An example by nature is nearly always concrete and fairly specific, and thus it gives the reader a kind of picture to look at instead of an invisible idea that he must juggle in his brain. Remember how back in the earlier part of the book I introduced Step 2 and said that its three sentences were to be about the whole of the sentence in Step 1, not just part of it? At that point my statement was very vague, very unclear in your mind. As a matter of fact, I have often presented that step to my classes and then deliberately stopped and waited. Sure enough, after a moment some brave student always raises his hand and says apologetically, "Could you give us an example?"

It is the most typical and soundest of human instincts to want an example. When I gladly give my class the example I gave you, they understand, just as you understood. Ponder that as an instance of the remarkable power of an example. It is like a flashlight focused suddenly on a page that you have been trying unsuccessfully to read in a room lit only by moonlight.

Remember, your ideas are clear to you, so you may assume that they're equally clear to the reader (after all, you've stated them in clear words, and the reader is presumably as intelligent as you are). But your ideas are clear to you not only because you have thought them out, but especially because you have accompanied them with pictures—examples—in your mind, and may in fact have derived them from concrete, specific realities (such as examples are). Those ideas, then, even though it seems to you that they *have* to be clear, are *not* clear to the reader—at least not as clear as they could be.

Therefore, like any other successful writer, you say at once, "For example. . . ." For easier ideas ("My grandfather is neat"), a succession of little instances will suffice ("He steps into clean clothes"); but for harder ideas ("Being cannot be defined"; "A falling body increases in acceleration 32.17 feet per second per second"; "Friction produces heat"), longer, more elaborate examples are necessary.

Assignment

Make five statements that a person younger than you might not understand without an example, and follow each with a carefully thought-out example. For instance:

> Friction produces heat. Rubbing your hands together is an example of friction; and if you keep rubbing them fast you'll feel the heat.

In this section, though I want to enlarge on one or two matters, I will be in fact insisting on the key instructions of this chapter. So first let's re-examine the all-important Step 4.

STEP 4

Make the material in the four or five sentences in Step 3 as concrete and specific as possible. Go into detail. Give examples. Don't ask, "What will I say next?" Say some more about what you have just said. Your goal is to say a lot about a little, not a little about a lot.

Most students will ask, "What about sentences X, 1, 2, and 3? Are they supposed to be concrete and specific, too?" No, that's the very point. Sentences X, 1, 2, and 3 by their very nature tend to be general and sometimes abstract. By their very nature they tend to be general because, after all, they summarize what is to follow; and a summary, being brief, tends to be general because specific details take up space. And by their very nature sentences X, 1, 2, and 3 are sometimes abstract because in them the writer is presenting his *ideas*—and as we said before, abstractions are precisely that: *ideas about things* (for example, *coldness, speed, beauty*); whereas the concrete is the realm of *things themselves (snow, racing car, girl).*

I say it's the very point that sentences X, 1, 2, and 3 must be general because to be understood, to make a point, you have to make brief statements ("Power corrupts: it corrupts the powerful; it corrupts the powerless; it corrupts every relationship between the two"). But those brief statements, precisely because they are brief and general, and sometimes abstract, do not register sufficiently with the reader: they are not *real* to him; they are not as clear as they could be; they are not deeply convincing. They need details.

This, then, is the very function, the very purpose, the reason for being of the four or five or ten sentences that follow sentences 1, 2, and 3: to bring the briefly stated abstract and general notions of sentences X, 1, 2, and 3 down to the concrete and specific, down to details.

This is a good point to do what some of you have been eager to have me do: give sentences X, 1, 2, and 3 their traditional names. All right: sentence X is called by a number of names: theme sentence, thesis, thesis statement, central idea, main idea, or simply theme (from which a composition called a theme gets its name). Sentences 1, 2, and 3 are, as far as I know, always called topic sentences. And the topic sentence together with its four, five, or more sentences (often called material, support, development, or specifics) is called a paragraph.

We've already solved the puzzling old question, When do you begin a new paragraph? haven't we? It's simple: you begin a new paragraph when you are finished providing the examples and the other concrete, specific details for one topic sentence and move on to the next topic sentence. And you already have all your topic sentences; they're sentences 1, 2, and 3.

Notice that the sign to the reader that you are beginning a new paragraph is (a) dropping to the next line and (b) beginning that line with an indentation at the left. Let me caution you that, while every new paragraph begins with this indentation, not every indentation *in what you read in print* begins a new paragraph! An editor, or the writer himself, may within a single paragraph add one, two, or even several indentations, so that a single paragraph *looks* on the printed page like two or three paragraphs. The reason for doing this is to make the page look more inviting to the reader, who is dismayed at the sight of a page of solid type; to give the reader more frequent breathing spaces, invitations to swallow what he has bitten off before he takes another bite. That breaking up of paragraphs by additional indentations has been done frequently in this book.

But let me add two more cautions. First, *do not add extra indentations yourself!* Make *no* indentation until you come to a new topic sentence; if you do, you will lose your grip on the important sense of paragraph structure that you have now acquired. If later on you write for publication, you may wish to add extra indentations, or allow an editor to do so. Second, because what look on the printed page like paragraphs are often not whole paragraphs—as well as for other reasons—do not rely on your reading to teach you about paragraphs; learn about them by actually building them yourself according to the method you are studying here.

But you may say, ''Then why bother with paragraphs, if, as it seems, a writer or his editor can indent just about anywhere?'' The answer is that *paragraph* in printing means a block of type indented at the beginning. But *paragraph* in composition—even if it were not indented—means a unit of thought, and we can no more write, in the proper sense of the term, without strict regard to paragraphs than we can make a coat without cutting out all the pieces according to patterns.

Assignment

It's time for an assignment. This one will be connected not with the material we have just studied, but with Step 4 in general. What I want you to do is to write six or more pairs of sentences. The first of the pair is to be in general, even abstract, terms; the second, the same idea in specific, concrete terms. Here are a few examples:

> Some students are guilty of putting things off. Ted Jenkins, like other students I know, is always telling Dr. Gaetzmann, his chemistry teacher, "I'll have it in next Monday" and then scrambling to get the chapters on the Civil War read for his history test the next day.
> In her room I noticed two books. On the small table near Jessica's plaid easy chair I noticed Heller's *Catch-22* and Galsworthy's *Man of Property.*
> If he didn't have a job, he could study more. If Joe Greenberg didn't have to work thirty hours a week as a checker at the Spend-Easy Supermarket, he would have more time to study his chemistry and calculus.
> Because of transportation difficulties, there will be a delay in the delivery of your order. Because two of our trucks broke down, we can't get the eggs to you until tomorrow.

F

What, then, is the function of the paragraph? If writing seemed to you, before you began to study this book, a process of putting down one thought, then thinking of another thought and putting it down, then racking your brains to think of still another, then a paragraph, for you, meant an indentation marking some greater break in thought than occurs between sentences. But now you know that a paragraph is a group of sentences whose only function is to provide specific, concrete details for the thought expressed in its topic sentence.

While you are adding details, you must be on your guard against introducing new ideas into your paragraph, for the paragraph must be kept busy expanding on the first idea (that is, the idea contained in the topic sentence). Any other idea must, therefore, begin a paragraph of its own. Look at this piece of writing.

> Keats was clearly a Romantic writer. He had very little schooling and died young, but his Odes are among the finest poems in the language. Though his work contains some sadness, its dominant note is cheerful

optimism. His poems reflect his admiration for the work of Milton. Fittingly, he is buried near the poet Shelley in Rome.

Apparently somebody thought of this as a paragraph. I can assure you that it is typical of some of the "paragraphs" a professor of English literature gets from his students. There is more than one thing wrong with it, but I want to point out here only one fault, which is probably the root of all its faults. That fault is this: from one point of view, there is no topic sentence. What at first reading looks as if it might be a topic sentence—"Keats was clearly a Romantic writer"—is not a topic sentence at all, as proved by the fact that not one other sentence in the paragraph has anything to do with Keats's being a Romantic writer. Each sentence is about Keats all right, but not about the fact that he was a Romantic writer. Remember Steps 2 and 3?

From another point of view, *all* the sentences in the piece are topic sentences! And each one cries out for explanatory details that ought to be provided in a *real* paragraph of its own. For instance, how is it clear that Keats was a Romantic? We should expect to find a reference to the fact that he wrote, for example, about the romantic long ago (especially the medieval and classical past) and far away (for instance, Greece and Provence), and we should expect that reference to be made more specific by brief quotations from his poems, or at least definite references to specific poems. And that would be only one of the familiar traits of the Romantic poet that Keats exhibited; in fact, "Keats was a Romantic poet" would provide a sentence X for a theme at least three paragraphs long that would take the student a good hour to write. And nowhere in it would there be room for any of the other of the four ideas contained in the original paragraph!

Let's take the second sentence of our piece on Keats and show that it too is (I mean, of course, should be) a topic sentence. The specific facts, I believe, about Keats having little schooling and dying young are that he was taken out of school, apprenticed to a surgeon, and trained to be an apothecary, but died young. How young? How young is young? Isn't it a fact that he died at an age—twenty-six—when no other major English poet had produced anything worth remembering, and still, on the strength of the "Ode to a Nightingale," the other great odes, and "Eve of St. Agnes," attained rank with the other major English poets—Chaucer, Spenser, Shakespeare, and Milton? And that is only the beginning of the support that the writer's second sentence demands—a paragraph of its own, at least. And a sentence that demands a paragraph of explanation is clearly a topic sentence.

Keats, by the way, had an idea that he was going to die young; and that nagging thought might have discouraged him from trying to write at all. But he did write, and rather cheerfully. I mention this because, besides referring to or quoting some of Keats's lines on dying young, the writer of the piece, by including this, could have connected his assertion about "died young" logically and gracefully to his next assertion about "cheerful optimism." For another glaring fault of the piece is that its sentences, besides not being connected with any one topic sentence to which they could all contribute, are not, at least visibly, connected with one another. (True, they're all about Keats, but the reader doesn't see how this fact about Keats is connected with that fact about Keats, nor with the third and fourth fact.)

I suppose the part about Keats being buried near Shelley could be connected to the first sentence because Shelley too was a Romantic and lived at the same time as Keats (there is a more particular reason, but no space to discuss it here). The sentence on Milton could enter by way of contrast with "Romantic"—Milton was *not* a Romantic—because Keats imitated him. But the writer, we note, supplies no specific evidence. And so on.

True, we could imagine the piece on Keats as a quick answer to one question—"Say something about Keats"—out of ten in a surprise quiz. Even then, though it would not be very bad for that purpose, the sentences should perhaps be better connected. But *connectedness* (coherence) is something we will take up later.

Right now, there seems nothing left for this chapter except to point out a particular kind of example called an *anecdote.* This is a little one-or-two-sentence story. There is an example of an anecdote—the daring rescue of a little girl from a flaming building—in this chapter (see pages 34–35). An anecdote is a story that provides an example, an instance, an illustration. The anecdotal method is effective and frequently used. One magazine with a very wide readership clearly prefers, I notice, articles that begin with an anecdote (real or manufactured), and I suspect that a recent speech by a member of the United States Senate captured wide attention because it began with a number of anecdotes.

Obviously, it would be a mistake to use an anecdote so lengthy that readers would tend to forget the point it was supposed to illustrate, or so lengthy that room would be left for little else. It would also be a mistake to use too many anecdotes, with few or no other kinds of example and detail. But if you avoid these mistakes, you will find the use of anecdotes easy and profitable. Repeated warning: don't make anecdotes your only, or even your favorite, method of completing Step 4.

SUMMARY

In the body of the paragraph (the four or five sentences of Step 3) be specific: *Joyce Carol Oates's newest novel,* or at least *a best seller*—not *a book; an African Violet*—not *a flower; glazed doughnuts*—not *food.* Be concrete: *breaking shop windows and over-turning cars* to accompany the abstract thought *violence; white stone spires soaring into the blue sky* to go with *beauty; buzzing flies settling on the fetid remains of a dead hawk* to go with *ugliness.* Sentences X, 1, 2, and 3 are the place to be the opposite—general *(flower)* and abstract *(beauty).*

Go into detail. You assert that Beulah is disorderly? Give details of her disorderliness: the single beige stocking hanging out of a drawer, the sticky glasses and cups all over the kitchen, the botany notebook pages lying among discarded sections of yesterday's *Daily News.* And *be generous* with your details. Give examples. A profession is work, the primary purpose of which is not making money? Explain a doctor's or a clergyman's purposes as an example. These are the ways that you get decent *length* to your theme without using weak repetition and without racking your brain over what to say next.

Assignment

Write a theme on the following sentence X: "A student must have a regular schedule of study."

First, *study* here means what we generally call homework. Second, *schedule* (please notice how it is spelled) refers to time, not place or condition, so the quiet room, the study lamp, and so on, should be brought in only incidentally—certainly not as sentence 1 or 2 or 3. Third, if you disagree with the statement in this assignment, imagine yourself, for this assignment at least, to be an average student who does need to study regularly. Anyway, you need not agree with the material in *this* assignment.

Remember the form you are to use in writing your theme down on the page (see page 26). Remember that sentences 1, 2, and 3 must be about the whole of sentence X. Remember that you must have at least four or five sentences each after sentences 1, 2, and 3.

But most important—*because this is what the assignment is for*—be concrete and specific, far beyond what you feel necessary. Go all-out in this respect. Go into detail. Give examples. Don't feel ridiculous. You are not expected to produce a "good" theme here; but you can make it a good exercise.

CORRECTING
THE PAPER

We will not take up a new step in this chapter, for before we go on we must carefully go over the assignment you have just completed. The best way I can help you correct your theme at long distance is to present here a theme more or less like yours and indicate what is good and what is bad about it. Then you can say, "Oh, I made the same kind of mistake," or "Yes, I can see what's wrong with *his*, but I didn't do that kind of thing" (good for you). Very well, here's the theme.

X A student must have a regular schedule of study.
1. Time must be set aside for study if there is going to be any time.
2. Often, only time to be filled provides the necessary spur to study.
3. Only time set aside will make study a serious profession.

— —

X A student must have a regular schedule of study.
1. Time must be set aside for study if there is going to be any time. During vacation, for instance, a student finds his time filled up with a number of things. During the school year he would find many of the

same or similar things filling each waking hour, except for classes, if he didn't set aside certain hours for study. So without those hours he would reach the end of each day with little or no study done, because he had been "too busy." People, to, might take up his time if he didn't have hours when no one could see him.

2. Often, only time to be filled provides the necessary spur to study. Sometimes a student is tired, and only the fact that he has contracted with himself to spend an hour on the study of a certain subject will give him sufficient reason to go on. Sometimes he finds some part of the material too boring, but if he asks "Why study this?" his answer can be that he has that hour to fill up and he may as well spend it on that material. In both cases there is the temptation to turn to something else, but if he has agreed with himself to devote certain hours to study, he will not do so. If a lesson is too short to fill the hour, the extra time will give him sufficient reason to do the review, the extra drill, or the suggested extra reading that he knows he ought to do.

3. Only time set aside will make study a serious profession. Though for various reasons a person may have to be a part-time student, he will not be a serious student at all if study is just a hobby he turns to at odd moments. The hobbyist is satisfied with little effort and little accomplishment; only the person who dedicates a real part of his business day

to study and thus invests a real part of his life in study gives himself seriously to his work, expects something out of it, and can count himself a real student.

Yes, a regular period of study is the best tutor to keep a student at his tasks.

Well! Whoever wrote this theme seems to be fairly bright for his age: his ideas happen to be good, I think, but more to the point here, his sentences 1, 2, and 3 are really and truly about sentence X. Similarly, the four or five sentences following the topic sentences (sentences 1, 2, and 3) in each paragraph stand the test—that is, they are clearly about the whole of their topic sentences. The length, too, is good: about 380 words. I notice even that the writer's nice, short rounding-off sentence at the end neither just repeats sentence X on the one hand nor changes the subject or introduces a new topic on the other, but sums up what the writer has said about sentence X.

Let me pause here to say that *you* may, in your paper, have written three quite different topic sentences. Your sentences 1, 2, and 3 may have said, for instance, something to the effect that a student must pick certain hours in which he knows he is going to be free, must spend the whole time—except for a ten-minute break each hour—studying, and must stick carefully to his schedule despite temptations and the urging of friends. Or perhaps one of your topic sentences warned against devoting more time to easy or favorite studies and less time to difficult or less interesting studies. Again, one of your topic sentences may have been a caution to give some time in the schedule to each and every subject, in proportion to the amount of homework ordinarily needed for each (accounting classes require more homework than English classes, for instance). Or you may have had a sentence on flexibility, saying that if an assignment for one class is brief, the extra time can be used for part of an unusually long assignment for another.

Good. You see what scope for originality and individuality (creativity, if you want to use the word) a seemingly very rigid method affords—even when sentence X, the key sentence, is assigned and is the same for everyone. In fact, there is enough variety possible for two hundred students each to write on the same sentence X and not duplicate one another.

Of course the sentences 1, 2, and 3 you thought up are different! And the only test you need to apply to see whether your ideas are any good or not is to ask yourself whether sentences 1, 2, and 3 are actually, honestly about the whole of sentence X. Though I can't see your paper, I suspect they are.

But to return to our criticism of our anonymous theme, we have indicated that it seems well thought-out, well put-together. But though we cannot accuse the writer of putting down on paper just vague generalities, he has clearly not caught the real spirit of Step 4, has he? He has been concentrating on his *thought* (and that's certainly praiseworthy in itself); but that is perhaps the reason he hasn't also given *full consideration* to Step 4.

To understand this thoroughly so that you can detect and correct similar weaknesses in your own paper, you must go with me from point to point of our sample paper, from beginning to end. (You understand that this will be not an analysis of the theme, but an analysis of the fact that the theme is a violation of Step 4.)

First, paragraph one: "a student"—not bad, but couldn't the writer have been more specific by giving "a student" a name? *John Swenson* or *Karen Swenson* would make a stronger, brighter, more vivid picture in the reader's mind. I will not urge here the use of *blond, lanky, six-foot John Swenson,* because, though it's far more vivid still, it's a little rich for most of the writing your career will demand of you. But I do think John—the student—should be further identified. A high school senior? A college freshman? A college math major? This, notice, is a simple process of reasoning as follows: *student* is fairly general; the rule says I am to be as specific as possible; so I'll at least change it to something like *a college math major.* True, what I'm saying is true for all students, not just college math majors; but I am using—and can introduce—a college math major as *an example.*

"His time filled up with a number of things"—good, as far as the idea goes. This is all the *information* the reader needs. But the information isn't alive to the reader because he doesn't *see* it—or sees it, so to speak, only dimly, in the far distance. And by the way, isn't *things* almost the most general word you can use? So let's at least say that this student's mornings were taken up with swimming, reading the sports page in the *Daily Clarion,* and shopping at the supermarket for his parents; his afternoons with chess or tennis and working on his car or riding his motorcycle; his evenings with going to the ball game, watching television, reading, or visiting his friends.

"Well! Isn't this getting a little long?" you ask. It is. And not just with more words, but with more *things.* This is legitimate length; this is how you get length; and we are *not* playing see-who-can-write-the-shortest-theme. Does this objection come, perhaps, from the young man who after writing a couple of dozen lines said, "I can't think of anything more to say"?

But you have another objection. "All our practice in Steps 1, 2, and 3 amounted to sticking to the point. And I can see how you *should* stick to the point. But all this stuff is not sticking to the point. The *point* is that the student found his time filled during vacation. What filled it is beside the point."

An excellent objection that deserves not only one answer but four! First, it is true that to say "During vacation a student finds his time filled" satisfies the reader's *logical* needs; but it does not satisfy his *psychological* needs. He can say "I understand it," but he can't say "I see it" or "I feel it."

Second, by specifying, a writer can imply something beyond what he says, yet to the point. In this case, by specifying swimming, tennis, chess, television, and so on, he has implied that the student's time in summer vacation was not wholly taken up with essentials like eating and sleeping, but with occupations that could be eliminated or cut down.

Third, I think it's important to see that the details, though not essential to the writer's point, aren't really off the subject. Things one does during vacation are part of the writer's point, and *chess, tennis,* and so on are just another, more specific way of saying that. Just as important to see is the fact that if the writer began to talk a lot about the student as a chess player, he would be going off the point; chess then would *become* the subject, instead of just contributing to the real subject—namely, summertime occupations.

Fourth, in a somewhat similar way the law of diminishing returns begins to operate in Step 4. For readers' logical needs, a bare statement of the idea is sufficient, but because of their psychological needs, a writer makes generous use of details, specific and concrete material, and examples. But the writer can go beyond the bounds of generosity—in fact, beyond the bounds of common sense. Common sense must guide us in deciding the question, When does the number of details, the degree to which I become specific, stop being useful to the reader in giving him the picture I want to give him? It is time to make the point that the *as possible* in "as specific and concrete as possible" in Step 4 means not only "as far as you are able" but also "as far as you can without going beyond the bounds of common sense and hindering rather than helping you to achieve your purpose."

CORRECTING THE PAPER

So to list *playing tennis with his neighbor Jim* among the student's summer activities might not be going too far, but adding the location of the courts probably would, and giving the whole roster of opponents—Jim Jackson, Mary Rizzo, Nancy Chan, Herb O'Brien, Willa Mae Washington, Sally Yamafuji, Alicia Rodríguez, and Hank Feder—certainly would. Of course, after a while experience in writing will begin to guide you in this matter, as well as experience in reading, if you watch to see how other writers use specific details.

Did *you* exceed the bounds of common sense in your paper? Happy fault! That's all right, because you were told to go beyond the necessary, to go all-out. As you know, in learning something new we often have to exaggerate our motions. My fear is rather that you didn't do enough—like the anonymous writer to whose theme we must now return.

"He would find many of the same or similar things filling each waking hour"—why not say something like *When school reopened, tennis might give way to skiing and the sports page to football, but there would still be recreational activities to take up his time?* (I like the wording of "filling each waking hour," but I'm willing to sacrifice it—in this assignment—in order to be more specific.)

"Certain hours for study"—that is what this theme is all about, isn't it—a schedule? "Certain hours"—*what* hours, for example? Neither here nor elsewhere in the anonymous paper do we get a sample of this student's schedule, of his "certain hours." I wouldn't recommend—in this particular theme—a complete schedule (though if you included one in your theme, good; for you may have used it as one way to go all-out). But, as I say, since this is a theme on schedules, we should have at least a sample. What hours on what days did he set to study what subjects? We could say, *For instance, Tuesday and Thursday evenings from seven to ten he set aside entirely for chemistry. . . .*

"With little or no study done" could be *with his French untouched and only two of ten chemistry problems done.*

"People, too, might take up his time"—*what* people, specifically? And how would they take up his time? Again, it doesn't matter logically, but it does matter psychologically. What will be realer, clearer, more convincing to the reader is the specific statement that Joe Allen comes in without knocking and wants to spend an hour describing the neat motorcycle (make?) on sale at Clifton's.

At this point, however, it may occur to you to remark that we are asking the anonymous writer to sacrifice the dignity and formality of his original theme. To that extent, you may say, we are ruining it. It is certainly true that most pieces of writing the writer—and you—will be called on to produce will demand a degree of dignity and formality. Such will be a letter informing an insured person that his change of beneficiary has been recorded, or explaining to a customer why his new adding machine does not require oiling; a memorandum to a supervisor explaining why at this point an engineer specializing in thermal conduction should be called in; a history paper on the various causes of the Reformation. And the anonymous writer has surely produced a dignified theme with a fairly formal tone.

But here are two answers to this problem. First, to produce a theme marked by dignity and a certain formality wasn't the assignment, was it? The assignment was to write a theme marked by concrete and highly specific content. Perhaps, therefore, the writer should have momentarily put aside his customary dignity and formality, which apparently got in his way.

Second, couldn't the writer have kept his dignity and formality by a different choice of example? Visitors *his* sort of student might expect would perhaps stop by with a chess board or ask him to spend some time explaining grammatical cases in Russian. Our anonymous writer, if he is careful in his choice of examples, can keep his tone elevated and give concrete, specific details at the same time.

The rest of the analysis—which I can now leave to you—goes in the same way. "Tired"—from what? "A certain subject"—what, for instance? "Some part of the material"—what part of what material? "Turn to something else"—*what* something else? "Review"—of what? "Drill"—on what? But especially I would ask what some of the reasons are that a person "may have to be a part-time student." Does he have a job? Where? Doing what? Is she a mother? How many children? Of what age?

When the writer mentions "a hobby," I would give a trivial hobby or two as instances; but I think I'd then leave the last two sentences of this student's theme alone.

Assignment

Take *your* theme and go through it in the same way. If you are fortunate enough to have an instructor correct it for you, the corrections may take the simple form of *What? Who? For example? Be specific!* in the margins. (Correcting papers for this assignment is unusually long and tedious work.) Guided by such suggestions, but not limiting yourself to them, go through every sentence of your paper, changing every term—if you can—to something more specific and adding examples where you can.

I say "changing" and "adding"—unless, of course, your instructor wants you to rewrite your paper, do not try to make your corrections look beautiful; write over what you have written, or even scribble down the changes and additions on a fresh piece of paper. It is the process of correcting we are interested in here, not the preparation of a neat-looking paper.

Remember the purpose of what you are doing—have you spoken simply of "homework" in your original paper? Isn't *homework* the most *general* term you could use and still be understood? (Just *work* would be misunderstood for the student's job as box boy at the Eat-a Market.) What if your teacher announced, "For your assignment for Wednesday, do homework"? *What* homework? Beware of words like *way, thing, something, somebody, a certain,* and especially *etc.* in your writing; they are the least specific of all.

Finally, be sure to *save* this paper until the end of the course. Don't throw it away; we may have further use for it.

Here is another matter. It's not one of our steps. But it's a rule that, if kept, will improve your themes surprisingly. And experience shows me that this is just the point at which I should introduce it to you. So don't be annoyed at the interruption. Like everything else in this book, it's intended to be of practical use to you.

The rule I'm talking about might be approached something like this: look over the theme you've just written for the special purpose of seeing whether, as you went along from sentence to sentence, you didn't say "students" in one or two sentences, then perhaps "student" in the next, and then, in another, "you" or "we." If you did, then study this rule: *as far as possible, keep the same grammatical subject throughout your theme.*

Let me explain. The grammatical subject is the person or thing that does something in a sentence—does something or is something, did something or was something. For instance, in "Einstein persuaded Truman to undertake the production of the atomic bomb," *Einstein* is the subject; it was he who persuaded. In "He was afraid that Germany might produce the bomb first and thus win the war," *he* is the subject;

he is the person who was afraid. And the same sentence leads on to another subject, *Germany;* for Germany is also doing (might do) something: "Germany might produce."

Keep to the same grammatical subject. That means start out talking *either* about a student *or* about students—or about you, we, I, or anybody or anything else. But then in every sentence you can, keep talking about a student, students, or you—in other words, don't jump back and forth from one to another. Of course, you can and should often call a student *he* or students *they.*

Let me give you an obvious example of *not* keeping to the same grammatical subject—the wrong thing to do.

> A student who is not wealthy ought to find a college with low tuition. In fact if students sat down and figured all the costs before they enrolled in college, they might avoid serious trouble. An expensive school is not necessarily a good school. In fact, what college gives you depends mostly on how seriously you do your work there, whether tuition is expensive or not. If we loaf through school, no amount of tuition paid is going to make much out of us.

Now there are three different grammatical subjects in that paragraph: *a student, students (they),* and *we.* Notice that in some sentences the change in subject was logical: you couldn't call an expensive school *a student* or college *he.* (But notice that the writer could have kept on with *a student (he)* if he had reworded the two sentences in which the subjects are *school* and *college.*) But in most of the sentences the switch in subject is quite pointless.

Let's reword the paragraph to get rid of the needless switches.

> A student who is not wealthy ought to find a college with low tuition. In fact if he sat down and figured all the costs before enrolling in college, he might avoid serious trouble. An expensive school is not necessarily a good school. In fact, what college gives a student depends mostly on how he does his work there, whether tuition is expensive or not. If he loafs through school, no amount of tuition paid is going to make much out of him.

I hope you can see that revising the paragraph to eliminate unnecessary switching of subjects has improved it. If you can't see it yet, I'll have to ask you, for the time being, to take my word for it.

Now the reason behind keeping the same grammatical subject is this: it gives the reader one target to keep his sights on and thus makes his job of reading simpler and less likely to be confusing.

But before we go a bit farther, I'll tell you a story to illustrate a point to which we must come. Here it is. Until about half a century ago people kept perishable foods and foods that they wanted to serve cold in ice boxes: insulated cabinets, the top sections of which contained blocks of ice. But about this time there began to appear the now familiar electric and gas refrigerators, which, being colder, preserved foods much better, and even had an upper compartment in which solids as well as liquids could be frozen. Large refrigerators were installed in food stores, and even some foods that had previously not been kept in ice boxes were stored in them. I can only guess how much food has been saved from spoilage and how many people saved from food poisoning since the introduction of electric and gas refrigerators.

But do you know what the reaction of some people was at the time? They said the new refrigerators were too cold! (I understand that some of the first *warmer–colder* dials were installed on refrigerators not because they regulated the temperature at all, but because they kept such people happy.) Some people object before they think, just as some people (perhaps the same people) form opinions before they think.

So naturally I have to deal with objections to everything I teach, including the rule that grammatical subjects should not be changed unnecessarily. "Keeping the same grammatical subject," our ice-box friends will object, "would be too monotonous; it wouldn't allow enough variety."

Let us deal with this objection. It rests on a basically sound but often misdirected instinct for variety—that is, beginners often want to change what should stay the same, while they leave the same what they should change. To be brief, it is not only all right but desirable to repeat key words. Repetition, in fact, is one of the first principles of art: in the course of a musical composition, a composer repeats a melody, a theme, or a phrase—sometimes, it seems, endlessly; in paintings an artist repeats both shapes and colors. So in writing it is quite desirable to repeat the grammatical subject. It is, after all, what you are talking about and what you must keep talking about.

Whatever monotony may result from repetition of the grammatical subject can be dealt with in three ways (to two of which I must add a caution). First, you can use pronouns: if you are writing about George Washington, you needn't call him Washington in every sentence; it will be very natural to call him, usually, *he.* Readers do not object to the frequent repetition of pronouns—*he, she, it, them,* and so forth—any more than to the repetition of prepositions—*of, for, with, by,* and so forth—or of articles—*a, an, the.*

Caution: pronouns are not always desirable. In a remarkable little book, *How Advertising Is Written—And Why,* by Aesop Glim, we find the advice to eliminate, as much as we can, all pronouns but *I (me), you,* and *we (us).*[1] Perhaps we can compromise by saying: *use the noun unless it strikes the ear as unpleasantly repetitious; then use the pronoun.*

Second, use synonyms. If, for instance, you are writing a book report or a book review, you may find that you are writing *the book* an unpleasant number of times. Let's say that at one point you have just written, "The book also takes up briefly the phenomenon of migration." Then you start to write *it,* but you realize that, though *you* know the *it* here means "book," the reader may think it means "phenomenon" or "migration." So you cross out *it* and write instead *the book* and then realize that the repetition of *the book* is unpleasant. So you use instead *the volume* or *the work*—a word that's different but clearly refers to the same thing (book). In other words, you use a synonym.

Caution: like anything else, the use of synonyms can be overdone. While you are at the library, look for a work by H. W. and F. G. Fowler in which overfondness for synonyms is ridiculed under the name of elegant variation.[2] Now at least if we do not have time (and in real life we usually do not) for a complete rewriting of what we have written, synonyms are usually the best way out of an unwanted repetition in a place where a pronoun would be confusing. But read the Fowlers' book and be warned against synonyms that are unnecessary, ridiculous, or fantastic.

Third, try a change of sentence length and form. As I said a few moments ago, beginners want to change what should stay the same, while leaving unchanged what should be changed. Specifically, they are likely to keep switching the subjects of sentences, but to leave all the sentences about the same length and to have every sentence begin with the subject (with the result, by the way, that far too many of their sentences begin with *the*).

What those writers should do is see to it that on the average every

[1] George Laflin Miller (pseudonym Aesop Glim), *How Advertising Is Written—And Why* (New York: Dover Publications, 1961), p. 69.
[2] H. W. Fowler and F. G. Fowler, *The King's English,* 3rd ed. (New York: Oxford University Press, 1958), pp. 184–89.

third sentence or so is notably longer than the others. Are you ready with your objection? "Can't sentences be too long?" you say. Yes indeed, and a person can have *too many* teeth; but I've yet to meet a person with too many teeth—or a student with sentences too long.

The way to get longer sentences is not, of course, just to put in more words; that's always bad. The way to do it is instead of putting every idea in a little sentence of its own, to combine related ideas into longer sentences. We can talk a little more about this later, but for the time being, perhaps one simple example will be enough. You might write: "I have a cat. Her name is Tiny. I got her when she was a kitten. Now she is old enough to be a nuisance." But you could (and no doubt should) combine all this into one sentence: "My cat, Tiny, whom I got as a kitten, is now old enough to be a nuisance."

Now what if you reduce the number of sentences required in Step 3 by combining your sentences in this way? There are two answers. First, it's better to reduce the number of sentences than to leave the sentences uncombined. Second, after reducing the number of sentences, you may wish to add additional relevant information to your paragraph, like further examples or a fuller explanation of your point—and those are all to the good, of course.

Can you go back to your old themes and here and there, in this or some other way, combine two short sentences into one long one? It will be excellent practice for you. Perhaps your instructor will ask the class to do this as an additional assignment and to bring the results to class for reading aloud.

When you combine sentences in this way you will often automatically do what you should also do—namely, vary the form of the sentences. Now regarding the form of sentences, your instructor may wish to explain to you about simple, compound, and complex sentences, and loose, periodic, and balanced sentences. Personally, I do not find that such explanations result in any change in students' writing. But perhaps your instructor can correct your themes, or you can do so yourself, for this one thing: *be sure every third sentence or so begins with something different from the subject.*

For instance, take the sentence "I usually avoid Fifth Street because it has so many stop signs." That begins with the subject, *I.* But you could take *usually* out of its place and begin with it instead; thus "Usually I avoid Fifth Street because it has so many stop signs." You could also put the *because* part at the beginning: "Because Fifth Street has so many stop signs, I usually avoid it."

Doing this is a simple, easy, natural way to get variety. You will find that it makes your themes much pleasanter to read and that it makes them seem more grown-up. In fact, it is an *excellent* practice—be sure to remember to do it!

I want you to watch out for something else in your theme. It is this (and I wish I knew how to stress it as it should be stressed): when you are writing the theme proper, do not use sentences 1, 2, and 3 as headings or subtitles! Sometimes I find students writing paragraphs something like this: "Coal-burning locomotives have all been converted to diesels. Formerly, all cross-country trains were pulled by coal-burning locomotives, but now they are pulled by diesel locomotives." The writer has simply repeated the first sentence of his paragraph in the second, the only change being the few more words added to the second. Obviously, he has thought of his first sentence as some kind of title for the paragraph and has thought of the paragraph itself as beginning only with the second sentence. No! Your sentence 1, or 2, or 3 is the first sentence of your paragraph. Then the second sentence should begin to explain it or illustrate it or whatever; it should read something like "The old coal-burners used tons and tons of high-grade coal daily" or "When in the long run the use of diesel fuel proved more profitable, the railroads. . . ."

You will have to watch out for this, since I notice students doing it even after they have been corrected. Remember that sentence X and sentences 1, 2, and 3 are not titles! They are as much sentences within the theme as any other sentence.

Assignment

Write a theme on a subject of your own choice, incorporating all the steps you have learned so far (you should be fairly familiar with them now). But in addition—and this is the point of the assignment—try to have in each sentence of the theme (or at least each sentence in the individual paragraphs) the same grammatical subject.

But also be sure (and you may have to do a little rewriting to achieve this) that one out of every three or four sentences is notably longer than the others, and that one of every three or four sentences begins with something other than the subject, even though it uses the same grammatical subject as the others: "*Hoping* it would rain," "*To* prevent inflation," "*Sometimes,*" "*In* the prison," "*Though* the treaty was sometimes disregarded."

Naturally, your theme may be a little stiff and clumsy. No matter—it's excellent practice. After you have finished, read a paragraph or two out of a book to see how the author varies sentence length and sentence beginnings.

A BREATHING SPACE

If you consider yourself a poor student writer and if you have no objections to the method of this book so far, we probably can excuse you from understanding and remembering this chapter. It is, frankly, somewhat abstract and general, and it demands a rather tiring attention to the line of thought. You will have to do the assignments, though; and I urge you to pay attention to what I will say in section A about introductions and conclusions and to pay strict attention to what I will say later about reading and about being "interesting."

But if you have an interest in writing or if you have objections to the method, brave the difficulties of this chapter; pore over it as you would a difficult chapter in mathematics; study it until you make it your own. For it will answer your most serious objections. Moreover, it will give you a sophisticated insight into the process of writing and improve your skills.

A

I hope you've gathered that in Steps 1, 2, 3, and 4 it has not been just good advice that I've been giving you. No, as I intend to show you now, what you have learned so far is how any theme *must* be written, in some way or another (and what you have learned here is the basic way).

First, I intend to show that Steps 1, 2, and 3 arise from the very nature of things. For consider that before anything else, your theme has to have a *point*. If it doesn't have a point, obviously it's pointless. The following account will illustrate what I mean.

Suppose that I told you that yesterday I left the library by the east door, went over to the Applied Arts building and entered it by the west door, then took the center staircase to the second floor. There I looked into Mrs. Bradley's office and noticed a French textbook on her desk. Finally I left by the south door, descended the outside staircase, returned to the library, and entered it by the south door.

Then suppose I took up the subject of composition again. "Why," you'd say, "what was that story for? Of course, I understood every word, yet I didn't understand what it was all about. What was all that about going out the east door and coming in the west door? And what did the French textbook on the desk have to do with it? Was all that to show us something about composition? I don't get the point at all."

Exactly. By being pointless (I purposely made it so), my recital about going out the east door and coming in the west door illustrates what we mean—or rather don't mean—by *point.* And the fact that you were instinctively looking for some point in my recital illustrates that point is what every reader or listener is looking for and that every composition must have one. In connection with themes, some books call point purpose; you may call it meaning; but I believe you may understand it best as point.

Very well. First of all, writing sentence X forces you at the very beginning of your theme to decide what your point is. That's of the greatest importance, because if *you* haven't decided what it is, certainly the reader will have difficulty in knowing what it is. Furthermore, if you haven't decided what your point is, how are you going to know what to write? (Conversely, deciding at the very beginning what your point is makes your course immediately clear—you know with certainty which way you have to go or which ways are open to you.)

Second, putting your sentence X—your point—at the very beginning lets the reader know at once what your point is and therefore lets him know at once what everything that follows is intended to add up to. That's what the reader has got to know in order to *read* in any real sense.

After all, the sentence "Industry increasingly turns from coal to other sources of power" does not necessarily go with the sentence X "Coal is being used less and less" unless we *know* that that is the idea it's supposed to be going with. For it could just as easily be used to support another assertion, "Industry is undergoing changes," or a still different assertion, "There is a future for atomic energy."

Similarly, the statement "Every thinker had a theory worked out in his mind" could be about the assertion "In the Middle Ages controversy was rife," or—a very different assertion—"Each of the Founding Fathers contributed something to the Constitution," or still another, "The early nineteenth century was an age of widespread idealism."

You had better read the last paragraph again, slowly and thoughtfully.

"But surely," you say, "in those cases there could be no confusion; the writer would have made it plain." Exactly. And *you* must make it plain, from the outset, what your point is. The way to do that is to begin with sentence X.

Let me deepen your understanding of the simple-seeming Step 1 by dealing with some other objections. To take one, even after hearing an explanation like the one given above, someone will ask, "But do I have to put it at the beginning? Can't I put it somewhere else?" The correct answer is another question: "Why should you want to put it somewhere else?"

The last reply I received to this was "To be creative." Well, if being different *for the sake of being different* is your idea of being creative, I can see your point. Wearing one brown shoe and one black shoe would make you different, too. Why don't you do that? If I appeared in class wearing my pajamas, I'd be different, certainly. Only I don't think my students would call me creative. They'd have another word to describe me.

But to come back to my question "Why should you want to do that?" the correct answer is "To serve my purpose." Very well. Since purpose must govern everything, if you cannot achieve your purpose by putting sentence X at the beginning—or even by putting it into words at all—well, you must do something different. What might your purpose be in such a case? Usually, to avoid presenting the reader at once with a statement he won't accept, a statement he'll reject so firmly that he will simply close his mind to all your arguments. (On the other hand, there is a school of writers called iconoclasts who love to confront the reader thus, deliberately.)

Very well. But remember three things. One, your *purpose* cannot be just to be different, which is simply eccentricity, or sometimes a mask for laziness. Two, your need to have sentence X somewhere else must be very great indeed if it makes you sacrifice the marvelous advantage of letting the reader know at once what your point is.

Third, you must realize that if you don't state your point at once, you must still guide your reader toward that point through a mass of material in such a way as to convince him that he *is* moving clearly toward a point, without his ever being wholly puzzled and without his

A BREATHING SPACE

67

getting the idea along the way that he sees your point when actually he is mistaken. To do that takes great skill. Do you have that skill? I certainly could not undertake to teach it to you here. You may develop it; but if you are going to develop it, certainly the beginning of the development will be getting the idea of point deeply cemented in your mind. And the best way I know to cement it is to get lots of practice in writing themes based on the method in this book.

You know, it may be good to point out to both students and instructors that many objections are raised by students not out of any real doubt, but simply as a way of expressing something that stands between them and a clear understanding of what is being taught. But other objections seem to arise out of a student's unconscious feeling that he has a wealth of writing experience behind him, that he has well-developed talents, or that he is, in fact, a kind of genius—at least, too far superior to have to follow the rules given to the common herd.

No, the young girl taking her first violin lesson and the concert violinist have to hold the violin bow in the same way (and incidentally, it is not the way that "common sense would tell anybody" it ought to be held; it is the way that centuries of experience have shown to be most effective). The only difference is that the concert violinist will hold it in the correct way *better* than the young beginner; he will not attempt to be *different* or feel freed from the rules given to the young girl.

Well, for another thing, it should be obvious that an instructor should not take such objectors at their own evaluation. If they prove their competency in their first theme, well and good. Personally, in my experience with students, excellent, fair, and indifferent, at the colleges and universities where I have taught, I have yet to meet a student whose first theme is at once well-unified, thoroughly coherent, and in its content satisfactorily specific, concrete, and detailed. Vigorous, graceful expression, embodying fine intelligence and sensitivity, sometimes yes; striking ideas firmly grasped and set before me with talent,.yes; but not unity, coherence, and detail.

But let's consider a somewhat humbler objection. "Well," asks someone, "shouldn't every theme have an introduction, a body, and a conclusion?" I don't know where this idea arose. It may come from a statement by one of the most brilliant men who ever lived—Aristotle—who in his *Poetics* explained that every tragedy—*not* theme, notice—has to have a beginning, a middle, and an end—*not,* notice, an introduction, a body, and a conclusion.

Perhaps, though, this idea came from observation of professional writers who in their first paragraph indicate how what they are reporting or conjecturing fits into the general body of knowledge or theory in their field. Or it may come from observation of writers in popular magazines, who, to help sell their articles, attract the fickle reader with some startling or provocative idea at the beginning in hopes that he will read on into an article about coal mining or oyster fishing—subjects in which that reader is not likely to be interested.

In any case, the general answer is no; a theme need not, and ordinarily should not, have an introduction and a conclusion. Why not? The correct answer is, "Why should it?" If an introduction is necessary, then of course have one. But do not have an introduction just for the sake of having an introduction, any more than you would flap your arms up and down three times before putting on your coat—it's pointless. Of course, if you must give your qualifications ("I worked one summer in a gold mine") if the reader is to accept you as knowledgeable and your material as authentic, or if there is some term or concept you must explain before you ever begin—if, in a word, you have some real need for an introduction, have one, of course. But be sure it is a need and not just "a good idea" or "a way to have a clever beginning." And make it just as brief as you can.

In fact, I find one of the main troubles with themes consisting of an introduction, a body, and a conclusion is that the introduction and conclusion are often far out of proportion to the body of the theme. A not overlong essay or article—say 2,500 words—that you have read and admired in a book of essays or in a magazine may have up to 50 words of introduction and 50 words of conclusion; and that is not disproportionate. But if you keep the same proportion, your theme of 500 words can have only 10 words of introduction and 10 of conclusion (since 500 is a fifth of 2500, and a fifth of 50 is 10). So, if you must have an introduction, the nearer it is kept to, say, a sentence of 10 words, the better.

Your theme, if it is under a thousand words, does not need a conclusion, certainly not a summary of what you've just said. Look at it this way: your theme is perhaps as long as a page in a book. Now would you expect to find a summary at the bottom of every page in a book?

Yet I agree that your theme does need a *short* rounding-off sentence. This is a real need, because without such a sentence the last thing a reader reads is a mere detail of the last paragraph. He is therefore bound to at least feel, if he doesn't in fact think, that you left off before you came to the end. At least psychologically, then, a theme needs a last sentence, which can be a repetition of sentence X, or some short sentence in which you manage to drive the point of the theme home. I'm sorry that I can't give you a better recipe than that; but I can point again to the rounding-off sentence at the end of the anonymous theme on "A student must have a regular schedule of study" (see page 52).

Very well, then. Do have a *short* rounding-off sentence. And do have an introduction, as brief as possible, if you can't avoid having one. At the same time realize that, in general, the very best introduction you can have is to tell the reader precisely what your theme is about—in other words, sentence X. Sentence X will lead the reader right into the theme with no foot scraping, pushing, registering, ticket punching, or price of admission.

Another question that arises in connection with Step 1 is, "Does what we call sentence X have to be a sentence?"

Yes, it does. Early in your education, perhaps as early as first grade, you learned that a sentence expresses a complete thought. But turn that rule around and you get a truth that you may never have thought of before. For if a sentence expresses a complete thought, anything less than a sentence is something less than a complete thought, with the result that we must say a complete thought is always a sentence.

Thus "Coal is being used less and less," since it is a sentence, is a *thought.* But *coal* by itself, which is not a sentence, is not a thought. That is, *coal* by itself (apart, of course, from designating the substance coal) doesn't convey *meaning.* In other words, it doesn't make a point.

If you're inclined to doubt this, just imagine that someone sends you a letter containing the single word *coal* ("Dear Jack: Coal. Sincerely yours, Robert E. Jones"). All right. What does your friend Jones mean? What is his *point?* There *is* no meaning or point to his letter. (You might guess that he means "Send coal," but you'd have no way of knowing whether you'd guessed correctly.) Even if he adds words (short of writing a sentence) and says "Black anthracite coal in Arkansas mines," he still has not reached the place where he has made a definite point. In contrast, if he writes and tells you "Coal is being used less and less," you may wonder why he has sent you the message, but at least it *is* a message; you *understand* what he has written; he has conveyed his meaning; he has made a point—mystifying though that point may be.

Very well. We have already discussed the idea that every theme must have a point (otherwise it is pointless, like my account of going in the east door and out the west door). We express our point in sentence X. And, as we have just seen, nothing short of a sentence can express a point. Sentence X, therefore, *must* be a sentence. And, of course, if it is to supply our whole theme with a point, we must use it *as a sentence.* If sentences 1, 2, or 3 could be about just something *in* sentence X—about just coal, for example—then there would have been no need for us to make sentence X a *sentence. Coal* would have been enough.

But that is not all. Since sentence X makes a point, it determines a way, or certain ways, that the rest of the theme has to go. We can therefore say of a *sentence* that it has a marvelous organizing power that nothing else but a single short sentence has.

Furthermore, you will find that the single short sentence has a remarkable *generating* power. If I propose as a sentence X "College is different from high school" or "High school is different from grade school," you are forced to think of three or more ways that those schools are different for your sentences 1, 2, and 3. Then qhen you have those—the topic sentences—you are forced to think of details, of specific, concrete material, of examples, to make your point real and convincing. Thus the original short sentence *generates* your whole theme.

You will find that with a little effort you will think of sentences 1, 2, and 3—your topic sentences—rather naturally; and moreover, you will recognize them as right for your purpose when you think of them. In contrast, if you tried to write about just high school, a number of random, perhaps vague and incomplete thoughts would come to your mind, none seeming righter to you than any other, none particularly demanding either to be written down or to be left out. That is because a mere term, like *high school,* gives the mind no direction, whereas a sentence points it almost at once in one or another very definite direction. In view of all this, I think we can honestly say that a theme that begins with—and sticks to—a sentence X practically writes itself.

In addition to proposing all this theory, and before giving you your next assignment, I have another practical point to give you—and argue for—regarding your sentence X. It is this: sentence X not only must be a declarative sentence (not a question or a command), but for your purposes here it should also tell us what *is,* not what should be. For instance, it should be "High school is different from grade school" or "Each ingredient of an alloy contributes a necessary quality," not "High school attendance rules should be less strict" or "Newspapers should be made more attractive to teenagers."

Why do I say that? True, the *should* variety of sentence X, which produces what we might call secular sermons, has resulted in some celebrated essays. If you want to, you may as well try to write some—on your own time. But writing that kind of thing is not the training you need at this stage in your career. For it is too often based on *theory;* and you must come to see that the most valuable thing you will have to offer is not the theories you can think up, but your own experiences, limited though they may be, and the facts that you have observed, few though they too may be. On those grounds, I think, a professor I know once said, "If a student wants to write on juvenile delinquency, have him write instead on a juvenile delinquent he knows." So I suppose that if a student wants to write on American newspapers, we might suggest something like the reporting of crimes on the first page of yesterday's *People's Tribune*—something obviously within his experience.

You are right if you deny that theories are without value. But theories that are proved valid by experiments, and experiences that prove to be practical nearly always come from those best acquainted with the facts; for instance, valuable inventions in the field of electronics can be expected only from those who work daily with electronics—and the theories on which they are based are always then subject, of course, to verification.

It is not young people alone who are thoughtlessly enamored of theories. I'll tell you an illustrative story. In the days when I was registered as a private investigator, I used to conduct what are called insurance inspections for the large American life and casualty insurance companies. Often the people I called on as an inspector would tell me at once "This is not the way the insurance company ought to do this at all; they ought to—" and then they would give me a theory, manufactured on the spur of the moment, and clearly seen by them as right. They never stopped to think that the insurance companies had developed their method of inspection through a fifty-year process of trial and error and knew very well what kind of inspection would produce the results they had practical need of in their business.

Do you want an example of that practical knowledge, just for fun? What facts do you think an insurance inspector should be most interested in when inspecting the premises of a small business that is applying for fire insurance? Things like heat conduits too near the wall, exposed wiring, employees who dump ashtrays into wastebaskets, or inflammables stored too near the heat? No. The first question in the fire insurance inspection of a small business is, "Did this business follow another?" And the second is, "If so, why did the other go out of business?" Only at the end of the inspection is there the blanket question "Are there any obvious fire hazards?"

Think it over carefully and you will see the point. Think about it at length and you will come to a good understanding of the value of theories contrasted with the value of experience.

Before concluding this section, let me give you a related warning: do not write themes that attempt to describe the bad state our society is in, what with catastrophic drug addiction, widespread alcoholism, rebellion of youth, decay of morals, inflation, pollution of the environment, and the threat of fascism or communism. Many uninformed books and articles have been written about all this; do not add to them. Moreover, the subject is too vast to allow you to get down to cases, to really specific details. And of course, such a theme really rests too much on theory. (If, say, you live on Lake Erie and have personally observed its deterioration, go ahead, of course, and write on that deterioration; or if you know one rebellious youth, go ahead and write what you know about his rebellion.)

Perhaps, to put the matter in a nutshell, I might say: do not write sermons. Now sermons, of course, as I have already said, are a quite respectable form of composition, and some quite respectable people have written them. But writing sermons is not the kind of practice you need at this point. And what I have mostly in mind are what may be called secular sermons: "People should drive more carefully" and "We ought to keep our yards cleaner"—the sort of thing, in a word, that you often see in the Letters to the Editor column in the newspapers you read.

Finally, regarding the *should* form of sentence X, "It's a lot easier," as a student once remarked to me, "to tell what should be than to tell what actually is." It is in the latter—telling what is—therefore, that you need training. And that training is training, mind you, for the kind of writing that your career in school and after school will demand of you.

Before giving you your assignment, I should give you the solution to what may still be a puzzle in your mind—the method of inspection of small businesses for fire insurance. Here is the way the insurance companies' thinking goes. If the business (say a coffee shop) followed another, and if the former proprietor went out of business because he wasn't making a go of it, there is a question whether the new proprietor will make a go of it. If he doesn't make a go of it either, he may not care very much whether he has a fire or not—in fact, a fire may be the most profitable way to liquidate his bad business investment.

But if the former proprietor was doing well and sold his coffee shop only to go into a larger one elsewhere, then the new proprietor may well succeed too. And if he is successful, *he won't want a fire.* A fire would keep him from his daily profits until he could rebuild, and it would lose him customers, who would meanwhile form the habit of going elsewhere. Moreover, though his insurance would pay for some of the fire damage, it would not pay for all of it.

So since a fire would hurt the proprietor severely in the pocketbook (and he knows it), he would have a sharper eye for fire hazards than most insurance inspectors could have. In the person of this proprietor, the insurance company would have a representative (so to speak) on the premises every day, a person who would be as much interested as the insurance company in preventing a fire. All this is not an opinion that insurance people dreamed up; it is the fruit of long experience.

I give this explanation at length because I deem it worthwhile to emphasize to young people that "what you'd think" an insurance inspector would ask and do is often very different from what long experience shows he *must* ask and do. "What you'd think," even though common sense seems to be on its side, is what we call an opinion, and it's worthless without experience or experiment to back it up. Young people, because they haven't much experience, sometimes fall back on opinions or theories. All right, that's natural. But don't take your opinions too seriously. Don't write on them. Take what *experience* you have and what *facts* you know and use them as the basis for your writing. The result may not be as important-sounding as you'd like it to be, but it will win you the respect of mature readers.

Assignment

Carefully make up a sentence X for yourself, and keeping in mind the requirements of Steps 2, 3, and 4, write a theme on it. Don't forget to add a short rounding-off sentence at the end of your theme.

The reading you do in your daily life can be of help in your writing. In fact, reading is obviously your contact with the *written* language. In contrast, what you hear—the *spoken* language—is different in several ways: it uses contractions *(isn't, wouldn't),* whereas in fairly formal writing—such as you are encouraged to imitate—you find the longer forms *(is not, would not).* It uses *can* for *may* ("You can sit down now"). And spoken English prefers "Who are you going with?" to "With whom are you going?" (Note that this book, to serve its particular purposes, is written largely in the *spoken,* not the written, language. For instance, it contains many contractions. And its vocabulary is fairly simple. But let me warn you not to take this book as a model. In fact, it is—as I told you at the beginning—not so much a book as it is a conversation.)

Written language uses a much wider vocabulary. If you haven't read much in your life, you'll have to face the fact that you'll need to use the dictionary frequently. (And obviously, when you write, you can't use words that you don't know. But the question of vocabulary would fill another book.)

What is most important in connection with our work here is that something written—something printed—has an *orderliness* that you will usually not find in conversation. It has paragraphs, as conversation often has not; it has details and examples that conversation often lacks; and it has a far higher degree of connectedness than conversation.

Yet at the same time, there is where the difficulty begins. Not everything you read is a theme, even a long theme; so of course not everything you read follows all the rules that govern themes. For example, in novels, stories, plays, and most poems, you will look in vain for a sentence X. It's there all right, but it is seldom *expressed.* A friend of mine wrote a whole novel on the sentence X "Power corrupts"; but nowhere in the novel did he actually *say* "Power corrupts."

Moreover, in the paragraphs—often not so much paragraphs as convenient divisions—of a novel, a story, or a play, you will usually *not* find topic sentences followed by specific development. In the description of a place, in a short summary of happenings that took place over a long period of time, yes, sometimes; but in paragraphs detailing action as it takes place, hardly ever.

I want to emphasize this because I find that students entering college from high school have often read a good many novels, short stories, and plays, but they have read and studied little if any nonfiction—that is, the kind of writing that they themselves have to do in themes. As a result, they are almost alienated from the complex logical structure required in themes—a familiarity with which is also required, it is important to note, in the successful *reading* of much nonfiction. (Sometimes students are alienated from almost any reading that does not have an immediate entertainment value; in fact, for them the kind of attention span required to follow a line of reasoning does not seem possible.)

But all that is another story. If students *have* read nonfiction, it has most likely been books and articles of *information.* And here I must point out the difference between an article of information and a theme by going back to Steps 1 and 2, where I indicated that a theme cannot be based on a topic, but must be based on a sentence, the whole of which the rest of the theme is about. The topic of our original example was coal; the sentence about the topic was "Coal is being used less and less."

Obviously, though, somebody has to be able to write *some* kind of composition on the bare topic of coal. For suppose a group of editors are preparing an encyclopedia for a publisher. Now naturally, one of the articles will have to be "Coal," because some users of the encyclopedia will want to look that up. So the editors search for someone who knows enough about coal to write an article about it.

Notice that you and I don't know enough about coal to write an article about it. And it's not only that we don't know enough facts; we are also ignorant of what aspects of coal can and ought to be treated. Nor do we know how much space, proportionately, will be most usefully devoted to each different aspect.

So perhaps the editors find a mining engineer (who may in turn consult a chemist, a sales manager, and other people in a mining company) who is able to write an article about coal. Then, depending on the size of the encyclopedia (which will govern, in turn, the size of the article as the size of a child governs the size of the shirt you buy for him), this writer may, I should guess (I am not going to peek, but you can), tell us how coal got its name and then give us the physical and chemical constitution of coal. This will naturally require him to distinguish among the kinds of coal broadly speaking; and since the kinds—as well as the coal itself—must have been produced by certain causes, he may then describe the forces and activities that led to the formation of coal.

Since, as the engineer will have explained, the forces that shaped the coal did not operate everywhere, he may move next to the distribution of coal and of its various kinds throughout the world (slate in one area, peat in another),with more particular information on its distribution in the country or countries the encyclopedia is written to serve; as well as the distribution of coal in the principal coal-producing countries.

I can see that after that he might have a choice of directions in which to go. His choice might be to say, in effect, "Here you have different kinds of coal at various depths in various soils in all these different places. Now the question is, How do you get it out?" So he tells us about coal mining, perhaps giving us a history of it with concentration on the present time, and describing the kinds of mining, the techniques used, and so on.

Next the writer may ask himself, "But why go to the trouble of getting it out?" So what he might write next is a short history of the use of coal, with concentration again on the present time. (This would include chemical use of coal tar in producing, among other things, dyes, medicines, and perfumes.) At this point in his article you might find, as part of his account, what is in effect a theme on the sentence X "Coal is being used less and less." In fact, you might find several themes, based on several sentences, along the way.

But my point—a very important point—is that for the most part the writer's selection and arrangement of material was not dictated by a simple sentence X and its sentences 1, 2, and 3, each extended with illustrative details. It was dictated by the nature of the thing itself—the topic he was writing about—coal. For if we turned to the article on tuberculosis in the same encyclopedia, we would find different *kinds* of aspect selected for treatment and a different method of arrangement.

True, in most articles of information we would find some or all of the following, in some form or other: definition; description; cause; effect; distribution; parts; operation; use; history; current status; opposing theories; and economic, legal, political, and social significance.

But the most that can be given otherwise as a recipe for such an article, whether on a whole or on a part of a topic ("Current Treatment of Tuberculosis"), is this: use one sentence X or more in the article *if you can;* use topic sentences for paragraphs wherever possible; always *go into detail* where space permits, especially where the reader will wonder about the details ("Coal is required in the manufacture of steel"—why? how?). For the rest, try to answer questions that will occur to most readers regarding the topic.

Try to be logical in your development, putting like things together, putting first things first, and connecting things where you can. Do not leave out essential steps in a process. In description, go from left to right, from top to bottom, from foreground to background—use some order that the reader can follow easily. If a time order is involved, go from the beginning straight through to the end; do not jump unnecessarily from 1914 back to 1900, then forward to 1920. Throughout, keep the reader in mind and be sure that he can follow what you are doing. Always keep him *aware* of what you are doing; for instance, if you *have* to skip back to 1900, *tell* the reader "here we must skip back to 1900."

A BREATHING SPACE

But this book does not really undertake to teach you how to write an article of information. My underlying reason for taking it up is to warn you that in articles of information you may very well *not* find a sentence X, and that in by no means every paragraph will you find a topic sentence.

Before we go on, let's make this a convenient, if not altogether logical, stopping place and have an assignment—this time a reading, or rather an *investigative,* assignment instead of a writing one.

Assignment

Go to an encyclopedia—or two or three encyclopedias for comparison—and see how it treats the subjects "Coal," "Tuberculosis," "Platinum," and your choice of one of the following: "Magnetism," "Gypsies," "Jefferson, Thomas," "Furniture," "Dolls," "Mysticism." You need not read all the articles; but see what aspects are taken up, and read a little here and there to note the use of details and to try to find a topic sentence or two.

C

You have learned that in articles of information you cannot expect a central idea—a sentence X—nor can you expect a topic sentence in every paragraph. But when you read articles in which the writer's intention is to make some *point*—articles written as you write your themes—then an ability to pick out the writer's sentence X and his topic sentences is useful and perhaps even necessary.

Why do I say that? Sentence X—in reading usually called the central idea—is, as we have learned, the point of the whole article. But if you can't put your pencil on a sentence in the article and say "This is sentence X—this is the central idea," then you can't show yourself that you really get the point of the article. You may know the meaning of every word; you may have picked up several pieces of information; but if you can't say what the point of the article is, you haven't really read it successfully, have you?

Similarly, you must be able to tell what is the topic sentence of each paragraph (if it *is* a paragraph, not a piece of writing broken off by indentation from another paragraph). Occasionally, I'm afraid, some writers of even the kind of article we are talking about try to get by without topic sentences—something you must never do! In that case, you must make up the topic sentence you would have written had you written the paragraph. It is always the point that the rest of the paragraph is adding up to. For instance:

> A pair of trousers, half inside-out, lay across the unmade bed, at the head of which one of the rain-soaked window draperies was tied back with a purple necktie. Paperback books were scattered in profusion on the dusty carpet beside the bed, some of them open and face down on the floor. The closet door, half closed. . . .

Can you state as briefly and simply as possible what point is being made in the paragraph you've just read—what all the details are adding up to? It's "The room was disorderly," isn't it? (Or the same idea in whatever words you want to put it.)

If you're deeply interested in writing, read some articles, pick out the topic sentence of each paragraph, and show how each topic sentence is connected somehow to the sentence X—the central idea—of each article. Be very patient with yourself as you do this. First of all, you're not experienced at it, and it takes practice—practice that will repay you as much as, or more than, any other single experience in your whole education. Second, it's not always easy; even highly experienced people have difficulty with it at times. Yet those people—and you— succeed with it not so much by having superior intelligence, but by taking pains—by rereading, rereading again, testing this decision and that, and analyzing. Third, it's sometimes not easy because the *writer* did a poor job of making sure that you would see what he intended as the central idea of his article and what he intended as the point of each paragraph.

Because of these difficulties it will be useful for you to have an instructor help you. His guidance may, for example, go something like this:

> You say you think the central idea of this essay is in the sentence "Most people seem convinced that we will always have war"; you think that the point of the essay is that we will never get rid of war. But if that's so, what about the writer's statements that in the twentieth century, for the first time, some people became convinced that there could be permanent peace; for the first time we witnessed cooperation among nations in humanitarian efforts; for the first time there was a League of Nations that, if it did not prevent war, settled some disputes and therefore prevented some wars, and later a United Nations with the same purpose; for the first time there were some agreements, though impermanent, to reduce armaments; for the first time there was such a thing as a "hot line." You know, one test of a choice of central idea is this: does it cover all the points in the essay?

A BREATHING SPACE

You may say that what the writer is saying is that the League, the United Nations, disarmament, and international cooperation have all proved too weak, and that thus, despite awakened hopes, we will always have war. Is the writer saying that, or is he saying the reverse: despite the conviction of many people that war is inevitable, despite the failure of hopeful beginnings (they weren't total failures), it is significant that after so many thousands of years of human history we have finally had, in our century, at least some *idea* that lasting peace is possible, that not just idealists but governments have for the first time made beginnings in the direction of peace?

What is the relationship of the two ideas in the essay—despite hope, failure; or despite failure, hope? Reread the essay and see what you think. Perhaps you will find that in the first part of the essay the writer presented the side of the argument opposite his in its strongest form, so that the reader would think there's no disputing it; then only in the second part did he attempt to show the weakness of that side and present his own side. That is a familiar way of arranging an argumentative essay, but it is sometimes confusing to inexperienced readers. (An experienced reader, seeing *"Most people* seemed convinced," would suspect that later the writer was going to give reasons why *he* is convinced of the opposite, or of something different.) See whether this isn't one of the cases in which a writer, to serve a definite purpose, delayed his sentence X until later in the theme.

Assignment

In a library, find a collection of modern articles intended for students. Choose a fairly short article that seems simple and in which you feel you can find the sentence X—the central idea—and the topic sentences of the paragraphs. Reread the article as many times as necessary for you to convince yourself that you *have* found a sentence that you can point to (not just an idea or a summary in your mind) that contains the central idea. You will usually—though not always, as we have seen—find the right one either at or near the beginning of the article.

Find also some other sentences that a hasty reader might mistake for the central idea, and prove to yourself that none of them *is* the central idea.

Next, reread all we have said in this chapter about topic sentences, and then try to identify the topic sentence of each paragraph in the article you've chosen. Do you have to supply any that the writer didn't supply? Are you sure you have to supply one in every case in which you think you do? The topic sentence may contain more information than is needed in a sentence 1, 2, or 3. But it *will* contain the general idea that the rest of the sentences in the paragraph are meant to illustrate, define, explain, give the causes or effects or parts of, prove, perhaps even dispute, or supply facts or arguments or statistics for.

Perhaps you are in a class that is using a book of essays or articles for reading practice as well as this book. In that case, perhaps the instructor will select one article for the whole class to use for this assignment. If he does, then students can compare findings in the following class session.

D

In this section I will take up a matter that is related to the whole writing process and is the subject, I find, of vast misunderstanding among students. It is a matter to which, experience shows, a good deal of time and space should be devoted. This is the obligation most students feel to be interesting and impressive in their themes.

As you gather from what has gone before, someone writes a theme in order to *explain* something to somebody. He writes an article of information to give somebody information, with perhaps some explanation along the way. For instance, I tell readers that coal is being used less and less and then proceed to show them that—or why or how—coal is being used less and less. Or I assert that power corrupts, and backing up my assertion with facts from past and current history, I explain why that is so and what the consequences are. Or in an article of information about coal, I give readers information about all the important aspects of that subject. Along the way I assert, for instance, that coal was produced when buried plants were subject, away from air, to the hot and heavy pressure of the earth above them, and I might then treat that assertion as a kind of sentence X and proceed with a more detailed explanation.

So in your own experience. Your history teacher wants to know whether you understand the causes of the Reformation; you show him you do by explaining them in your own words. Or your supervisor wants to know what you think of putting a different amount of tin in a certain alloy; you tell him what you think and explain why to him. Or you try in a bulletin to make crystal clear to a group of employees what effect a change in the tax rate will have on the amount of their paychecks, and why.

A BREATHING SPACE

So I have come to my point about being interesting and impressive. For if we agree that to explain or inform, or both, is the purpose of our composition, then we must agree that it is not our purpose to be interesting or to be impressive.

Let's take interest first and spend a good deal of time on it. What I have just said shocks some students. They—evidently like many other students—have it in the back of their heads that they are writing "to be interesting," or to entertain. Now I think to clear this matter up we had better try to get to the bottom of it.

For one thing, I sometimes wonder whether those students' former teachers have not had it in the back of their heads that their students were all going to be writing for professional publication. So, assuming that an editor looks for material that will interest the greatest possible number of readers, those teachers felt it their duty to teach their students to be interesting—by which they sometimes meant, I'm sure, "entertaining."

In fact, some instructors unconsciously assume that all their students are going to be writing *fiction!* For instance, some time ago I became acquainted with an English composition textbook that was advertised as practical. It did indeed have much valuable material, not available elsewhere so far as I know, especially for helping students to acquire a more adult style. But the more I advanced in it, the more I found by the author's selection of examples and choice of technique that he assumed that students using his book—and it was in widespread use—were going to be short story writers!

Now a little conscious reflection will show that not one person in a thousand (by my calculations) becomes a published writer. And most of even that tenth of a percent are under no compulsion to be entertaining in the work they do; they write explanatory and informative material, the readers of which would regard any substantial effort to be entertaining as ridiculous. Still fewer people publish fiction.

In other words, to make a long story short, students should be prepared for the kind of writing they are going to have to do. Because that is not fiction, nor entertainment of any kind, it has a purpose other than to be interesting. Students, therefore, should realize that they are practicing to present explanations and information to the history professor who is examining them for their understanding of the causes of the Reformation, to the supervisor who wants an opinion about a new alloy, or to the employees who want to understand a change in payroll deductions. None of these people wants "to be interested"—rather, *they are interested* in getting from the writer a clear understanding of something.

Sometimes instructors, who have to spend a lot of time reading themes, complain that they want interesting ideas from their students, instead of theme after theme on pets, sports, cars, bicycles, and pollution. Now I think we will all agree that students, when given a free choice of theme subjects, should move progressively away from topics that would interest only junior high school students. "My Cat," "My Dog," or "Our Trip to Yellowstone" will usually provide little preparation for the kind of writing that the student will have to do later. The student who chooses such subjects does not have the future in mind; he is concerned only with turning in an assignment.

At the same time, however, we cannot expect most students to be Walter Lippmanns, Loren Eiseleys, or Jacques Barzuns. Students can write only about what they know and understand. Instructors cannot expect them to write with the experience of a man who has been a newspaper columnist or a distinguished professor for twenty or thirty years. A decently unified, detailed, coherent, and clear My Cat theme is (though quite modest) a definite accomplishment—a far more promising performance than an incoherent, unsupported, poorly informed theme on communism or democracy.

Students ought to be encouraged—and ought to encourage themselves—to write, for example, on some lesson they have mastered in some other subject they are taking or have taken, or if they are employed, on some serious aspect of the work they do (so long as they do not write a process theme). Instructors must be prepared to read themes on plant taxonomy, carburetors, business cycles, tire trade-ins, abnormal brain waves, crop rotation, electrical circuits, and tariffs, whether they are interested in those subjects or not. For it is not their purpose, in reading themes, to be interested. Rather, they must *be interested* in whether or not the student is correctly applying the principles of composition to his subject matter, whatever it is, and in whether the student is progressing in applying those principles. Those instructors who can see only subject matter are in the wrong business—and they usually know it.

But students will probably still want to write on something "interesting." Once, when I assigned "College is different from high school" as a sentence X, one of the ablest student writers I have ever taught complained, "Must we write on something so dull?" Well, what is *dull?* A high school teacher who decides she wants to teach in college is asked by a college administrator who is interviewing her, "How do you see the difference between college and high school?" Then the "dull" subject becomes intensely interesting (not entertaining, mind you), for whether or not the applicant is hired just may depend on her answer. In fact, if a student has entered college or plans to go to college after finishing high school, he should be thoroughly interested in (not entertained by) that same subject, because his success will depend partly on his understanding of it.

Some of this section is directed to your teacher as much as to you. You can guess that from the language used, can't you? That's true of the following paragraph. But you read it too, because it's no harder reading than much of what you have to study in your other classes.

No, we make a mistake in being interested in the interesting. On the one hand, we can get students so highly excited about something that they will be eager to write about it. But their eagerness will not automatically—nor miraculously—teach them unity, coherence, and the habit of adequate support, for those things must be taught slowly, patiently, and systematically; and students will not be burning with desire to learn them. So while students may be eager to write on what they are excited about, I am interested in seeing what they do when they write not on some subject of intense interest to them, but on one with which, simply by being orderly and detailed, they generate moderate interest—for themselves and others—in what may seem to them ordinary or dull. For since most of the writing they will have to do in life will be on quite unexciting, in fact unpromising subjects, it is that kind of writing they must show themselves willing and able to succeed at.

Of course, if you the student were born to have an interesting way of putting things, good! If you were born to be charming, then charm will flow into everything you write. But we teachers cannot teach you those personal qualities. If we were to try, what we would produce is a phoniness that you yourself—not to mention others—would soon grow tired of.

What then? If you don't possess those personal qualities—any more, perhaps, than you possess naturally curly hair or perfect teeth—are you doomed? No! Such qualities as charm and wit should be highly valued, but they must no be overvalued. In fact, other qualities, like honesty, earnestness, diligence, and patience, can be acquired by anybody; when you practice them, they too will flow into everything you write. And to you personally, those other qualities, I'm willing to bet, will in the long run prove more important than inborn charm and wit.

Now before I move on to other things, I want to tell you an anecdote from my own experience, one that has to do with interest and that will leave you with another puzzle to work on.

Once I taught a graduate class in advertising. And though that was years ago, I still remember some of the well-known principles of advertising that made up my course. One of those principles we might approach in the following way. Say you're leafing through the pages of a magazine in a barbershop or beauty parlor or in your dentist's waiting room. Suddenly you stop because a particular advertisement catches your attention. Whether it is the picture in the ad or some caption or sentence in large type, it has captured your interest. Hoping that you will not be called for your turn in the chair just this minute, you read on down the page until you discover that it is an advertisement for lawn mowers. You may not be in the market for a lawn mower, either because the one at home is giving good service or because you live in an apartment and aren't responsible for cutting grass. So naturally, after a final glance at whatever it was about the advertisement that drew your attention, you turn the page, reflecting, perhaps, that the advertisement was a good, attention-getting ad that would stop anybody leafing quickly through the magazine.

Now advertising is—or should be—a very practical thing. An advertisement of the kind that stopped you should exist, and be paid for, for just one purpose: to sell merchandise (in this case, lawn mowers). So well do shrewd people concerned with advertising realize this that they have devised ways of measuring the actual selling power of any advertisement. One way they do it is to run a certain advertisement (say the one you looked at) in an edition of a magazine sold in New England but not in the Midwest, or vice versa. Then, making allowances for several variables like weather, they find out how much higher (if at all) their sales were during the following week in the region where the advertisement was run, as compared to sales in the region where it was not run. Then they try another advertisement and see how much more or less effective it proves in selling their lawn mowers.

Mind you, it is not in people's reading their advertisement that they are ultimately interested. Does the reader then buy a lawn mower? is the question they're concerned with. In your case, they simply provided reading matter—at considerable expense to themselves—while you waited for the dentist, and they got no return, except perhaps your unvoiced thanks.

Now here is the curious fact: advertisers who have measured the selling power of their advertisements have discovered that those advertisements that will "stop anybody"—as the lawn mower advertisement did you—sell *less* merchandise than advertisements that attract and are read by only those people who are in the market for the product advertised. Now why should that be? There's a puzzle for you to work on.

Meanwhile, however, learn a lesson from the advertising people: when you write a theme, assume that the person or persons for whom you are writing are already interested in the subject. Ignore other people—there's not much chance of your interesting them for more than a minute or two. And what's the point? If somebody's not interested in coal, why bother him with coal? About all you'll end up doing is annoying him; he doesn't want to know what you have to say about coal and is impatient with your bright beginning and the gimmicks you have dragged in to make your paper "interesting."

Remember the encyclopedia articles? Did they employ cheap devices to get readers to read about subjects in which they had no interest—coal, tuberculosis, or whatever? No, the writers of the articles assumed that a reader who would look up a subject would want or need to read about it, and they got down to the business of making it as clear as they could. No "When you see a freight train passing and notice among the cars those open ones loaded with coal, do you ever stop to think. . . ."

I suspect that the notion that in writing a theme you have to be interesting at all costs may be partially the result of students' having to read—or listen to their instructors read—their themes to their classmates. This public reading of themes has great advantages, but after many years I have decided (though I may be wrong) that it has, in the long run, greater disadvantages. I know that, for example, when the best themes are read aloud, many of the themes for the next assignment show sudden, marked improvement—that is, they show the effects of imitation and competition. Better *themes* are produced this way—temporarily—but, I'm afraid, in the long run, not better *writers.*

However that may be, among the immediate disadvantages of such public reading is that it may popularize the notion that how a writer's classmates react to a theme is the measure of its worth. That notion naturally makes attention-getting gimmicks and sophomoric humor seem desirable, with the result that the young writer neglects his proper purpose—explaining something—and seeks instead to be entertaining. Of course, if class discussion of a paper centers on clarity of point, clarity of connection, and clarity through the use of concrete detail, then that may be another matter.

Practically, therefore, what do you as a student do? Seek to amuse the other students? That might be good practice if your future career is going to be that of a gag writer for television comedians. Living as you do in a world whose heroes and heroines are entertainers—"stars," as they are called—maybe without really thinking about it you have it in the back of your mind that you too are called on to be an entertainer. No—no more than you are called on to pull your schoolmates' teeth, ticket them for overtime parking, wash their shirts, or repair their shoes. Lay down this unnecessary burden of being their—or anybody's—entertainer, of being "interesting."

Instead, in writing a theme seek to do a solid, sober, serious piece of work. That will gain you the quiet respect of your real friends in place of the noisy applause of those who would like your free services as a clown.

Assignment

Choose some subject that interests *you,* but that does not seem to have much interest for most people you know. It may be a hobby, a school subject, a form of recreation—anything. You may even, for this particular assignment, choose a topic that would interest only a junior high school student. Write a sentence X about it (decide carefully what that sentence should be), then sentences 1, 2, and 3 as usual, and then finally a theme.

Pretend that your reader *is* interested in your explanation. Do not be apologetic. Do not *try* to be interesting. Above all, *avoid all humor.* Do a serious piece of work. Do not suppress, of course, aspects of the subject that seem interesting to you; but do not try to coax imaginary readers to be interested in them.

This is a convenient place to take up the idea of *the reader.* After all, the reader is the person whom you might be tempted to interest or to impress. Let's bring this reader out of the shadows and get acquainted with him. He appeared several pages back when I remarked that a theme is intended to explain something *to somebody.* That somebody is your reader. If he is actually your history professor, a supervisor in your office, or your employee, then you know exactly who he is and can write accordingly.

But since what you are doing now is writing practice papers with no actual reader but your instructor, you are going to have to *imagine* some particular reader or readers. Of course, you can choose your instructor as the person for whom you are writing the theme. That's what most students do, and it isn't a bad idea, because the instructor is pretty much like most people for whom you'll be writing something outside your English class or outside college.

Still, that may not be enough. What I suggest that you do, therefore, is select some real person whom you know, then imagine that you're writing your theme to make something clear to him. This real person may be a boy or girl younger than yourself; he may be a relative; or he may be some other adult. He should *not,* however, be a classmate— too much temptation to be "interesting" or overfamiliar there! —unless he is a classmate you're used to doing serious study with and explaining things to. Keep this person in mind in every line that you write. Do not get so intent on your subject matter that you forget him.

Now the purpose of your doing this is twofold: first, it keeps before you the general purpose of all themes—namely, to explain something clearly *to somebody.* Let me illustrate that point. If I want to discuss with a linguist why in English we say "he *was*" but "they *were,*" I might simply talk to him of rhotacism, the change from an intervocalic *s* (Primitive Germanic *z*) to *r* as a result of the Germanic stress assimilation known as Verner's phenomenon.

If I were explaining the change in verb form to a linguistics student, however, I'd do it somewhat differently. I might say, "Sometime in the history of the English language, people began to pronounce the *s*'s that came between two vowels (including the vowel that is the now silent final *e*) as *r*'s. The *s* in *was* had a vowel before it but not after it; so it stayed *s.* But the matching *s* that once was in *were,* since it had a vowel before and after it, became *r.* You get the same thing in "he *is*" (which still has an *s*) and "they *are*" (in which the original *s* became an *r*). Why did *were* and *are* have a vowel after them? The vowel was part of an ending which, earlier in history, showed that *were* and *are* were plural.

That is to say, you learn to keep in mind that how you explain something depends on whom you're explaining it to.

Second, keeping a certain reader or readers in mind tends to keep your *tone* constant. You won't speak of an altercation in one line and call it a rumble in the next, or speak of juvenile delinquency in one line and call it "mixed-up kids fouling up" in the next—the kind of change of tone that gives the same unbeautiful effect as the sudden jump from bass to soprano we sometimes hear from a boy whose voice is changing.

So to repeat: keep a certain reader in mind as you write.

While we're talking about readers, the way you explain something to them, and the tone you use with them, perhaps you can see certain difficulties in the simple rule I'm about to give—namely, *do not try to impress the reader.*

Let's take up the difficulties first, then come back to the rule. The difficulties, as I see them, are three: first, I explained a short while ago that in talking with a linguist, I'd explain something differently than I'd explain it to a linguistics student; and you noticed that in speaking with the linguist, I used a different *vocabulary,* including the technical terms *rhotacism, intervocalic, Germanic stress assimilation,* and *Verner's phenomenon.* But while those words may have impressed you, I did not use them to impress *the linguist.* It's simply as natural for two specialists in linguistics to use the technical terms they're used to calling things by as it is for two carpenters talking together to use words like *joist* and *strut* (whatever joists and struts are—personally, I've no idea). The carpenters are not trying to impress each other! That's just the way carpenters talk.

The trouble is, you'll naturally think: "That's the way so-and-so, for whom I'm writing, talks—and, I suppose, writes. He presents difficult ideas and uses big words. So I suppose that's what he wants me to do. Probably nothing else will satisfy him."

No. The sort of person you have in mind (perhaps your instructor) will certainly want you to do your best and to be dignified in your way of writing. So don't use contractions (like *don't* for *do not*) as I do here. Especially, don't use *any* words that you feel are slang. In other words, doing what your reader expects you to do will probably come down to this rule: *do not offend the reader.* This rule puts to use the general rule of life "Try not to offend anyone on whom your success depends." "Of course—common sense," you say. But how often overlooked!

But otherwise, concentrate on explaining things clearly and forget about big ideas and big words. Deal only with ideas that are clear to you, and use only words that are natural to you. Otherwise, you won't be impressive. You'll be comic, in a way that you didn't intend. And the person you've tried to impress will be out of patience with you and will reject your work as worthless. You will come nearest to satisfying your reader if you do your *honest* best—that is, your very best can only be your attempt to be as clear as possible in language familiar to you. If you try to do *better* than your best, you'll land in the soup.

You do not write a theme in order to use fancy talk. While most students realize this, some of them have *got* to get it into their heads!

The second difficulty, though, is exactly this: some of what you read, some of the great works of literature that have been admired by generations of readers, are in a sense fancy talk. Or they may seem so to you. Lincoln wrote "fourscore and seven" when he could have written *eighty-seven,* the way he would normally have said it. Now we haven't time here to go into the theory behind this. Put practically, your question is this: "Shouldn't I be imitating those writers?" The answer is: probably not now.

Why? The explanation is that though the language in Lincoln's Gettysburg Address was unusual, *it was not unnatural to him.* Is it natural to you? Because it was natural to him, he knew how far to go without seeming to strain. He knew what *not* to do. And if he correctly chose the solemn *fourscore and seven* instead of *eighty-seven,* he also correctly chose the short and common *met* instead of the fancier words *gathered, assembled,* or *congregated.* Can you do that?

Maybe someday you can. The language that is *natural* to you will grow and develop and be enriched as you read more, write more, live more, and grow older. When fancier language becomes *natural* to you, then go ahead and use it (if the readers you have in mind will under-stand it, of course—otherwise, what's the point?).

But—reaching the third difficulty—you may argue that this de-velopment of yours, this growth, must take place, and how is it going to take place if you don't stretch yourself, if you don't strain? Very well. Some people reach a stage at which they become fascinated with words. Good! And, just as when a boy reaches an age at which he becomes fascinated with cars, he will not be satisfied until he drives one, whether he has learned to drive or not, so people at this stage with words will not be satisfied until they use them, whether they have a clear idea of what they mean (or any place to go with them) or not.

If you are one of those people, this is a passing stage you are in, and it has good reasons for being ("It has its *raison d'être,*" you might say). But it should be quickly followed by a stage in which you're willing to look the words up to see whether they're really the words you want.

Finally, I think we can sum up all we have said about being interesting and being impressive with this rule: *if what you write is a genuine effort to give a clear explanation by being orderly and detailed, it will have exactly the interestingness and impressiveness that it should have.*

STEP AGAIN

I find that some beginning writers—especially some who do not think of themselves as beginners—immediately protest against the rule that a writer should be as specific and concrete as possible. It would be interesting to discover the unconscious reasons for their protest. There are no *conscious* reasons. That is, they have never heard the rule before; they haven't thought it over; they haven't made any investigation into whether successful writers, including their favorite authors (if any), observe that rule. They haven't had *time* to come up with conscious reasons; they protest immediately.

It may be a common-sense reaction: why say my great-grandmother stepped out of her Stutz Bearcat when you can convey the essential information if you just say she stepped out of her car? That objection we've discussed, haven't we? Perhaps, though, the unconscious rejection of Step 4 springs from a suspicion that the rule is going to involve some patient work that human nature would rather shirk. In fact, when a young woman said to me, "Are we to assume that our readers are too stupid to think up their own specific examples?" my answer was "No, but they're too lazy."

Too lazy or too impatient, the reader is reading too fast to stop and think up examples for himself. For instance, if I say "One quality you see in professional workmanship is patterning" and then go on to my connected point "so you, as a writer, should use patterning too," the reader is going right on to my connected point with me. He isn't going to stop to think of the windows in his English classroom all made alike; the buttons on his new cardigan sweater all the same size and the same distance apart; the matching headlights, fenders, and doors on each side of a Stutz Bearcat; and the equal-sized planes on the yellow pencil lying before him on his desk (a desk that has four legs just alike).

No, the reader hasn't been trained to read that way. And the unfortunate result is that my point that patterning is a sign of professional workmanship makes little impression on him; he's not struck by it enough to be convinced; in fact, I'm not sure he really understands it. So since *he's* not going to think up the examples, it's up to me, the writer, to do it. It's the writer's business, not the reader's, to be specific, concrete, and detailed and to show connections. In fact, if you ask me, that *is* the writer's business: what his work consists of—and it is work—is showing connections and going into detail.

If you're a doubting Thomas, look into the reading you do to see whether the rule in Step 4 isn't one that all writers seem to be following. I'm going to refer to some specific examples here; you can look them up—or any others, since in one way or another all writers use Step 4. I'll leave the poets alone; since the concrete and the specific are their very bread and butter, you'd just say "Well, of course, poetry. . . ." (It's remarkable, though, how many students in creative writing courses think they are writing poetry when they are writing down *thoughts* instead of things: *sadness* instead of a bent head, a slowly twisted ring, a knotted brow, a sigh, or tears.)

But to go back to prose. Striking examples of the concrete and specific are to be found in Ian Fleming's James Bond novels. They've sold by the million, so perhaps you've read one—most people I know have. Why, by the way, *have* they sold by the million? I can think of a few reasons, but the one that concerns us here is that they contain outstandingly specific material. When Bond lights a cigarette, we are likely to get the brand name of the lighter; if he stops to eat, we get the menu, including the year and name of the wine; when he gets up, we may learn exactly what clothes he puts on, beginning with underwear. If Bond is near a woman (as he sometimes is), we often learn the brand of perfume she uses. Bond opens a bathroom cabinet and we get a catalogue of the toiletries contained—nearly all by brand name.

Now a successful and highly conscientious writer recently remarked to me that he detested the use of brand names as a way of being specific. I can well understand that. But he went on to agree that practice in being very specific may save students, when they write papers for their classes, from the tendency to write what are called generalities, generalizations, or unsupported generalizations. (And by the way, in rereading my friend's autobiography, published a few years ago, I find a number of brand names—Studebaker, Mennen, and Lucky Strike among them.)

But to get back to Mr. Bond and the details, including brand names, the author gives us about him, the point to notice is that such details have nothing to do with the story. Sometimes they help to show what kind of person some character is, but usually not. Well then, you may say, why use them? To help sell your books by the million is one quick answer. But the real answer is that Ian Fleming's scenes are above all things remarkably *clear,* and that capturing the reader's imagination with exact details contributes to their clarity.

STEP 4 AGAIN

Since nothing is better than an example, go to a library and take out one of Fleming's books and look for examples. And while you're there—if you're inclined to dismiss Fleming as "a popular writer"—go to the works of some of the outstanding makers of today's literature, writers like Flannery O'Connor, Graham Greene, Evelyn Waugh, Robert Penn Warren, and see whether you don't find the same thing.

"Well!" you may say, "you've picked out writers of fiction. A constant, generous use of the concrete and specific is their stock in trade. We're writing *themes,* remember." Yes, you are. The first and constant duty of a writer of fiction is to enable readers to pretend that instead of reading a story, they are really experiencing the events of the story—and this the writer does not only by making every event seem the result of a cause, but also by constantly feeding his readers' imaginations with convincing details. As a writer of themes you, you say, have no such duty.

True enough. But are you going to let your readers' imagination go to sleep while, you hope, their minds continue to plow right ahead through your generalities and abstractions? No, readers are not made that way. Their constant experience as human beings is of quite specific, concrete sights, sounds, smells, tastes, sensations of temperature, and so on. *These* are the basis of their daily thoughts. And even when they try to shut off the outside world and to work in their minds with abstractions—like justice, peace, prosperity, progress—their imaginations will *automatically* try to summon up pictures to go with those abstractions, often producing very vague pictures, sometimes just the look or the sound of the abstract word. Human beings don't think *with* pictures; but they never think *without* them.

It is into this fundamental psychology of readers that you must fit what you write. You must help—not ignore—the effort made by their imaginations to produce good accompanying pictures so that their thought process will go along as it should. So do not hesitate to borrow from the stock in trade of the writer of fiction. (He does not hesitate to borrow from yours; an astonishing number of short articles of information form parts of the James Bond novels.)

Still, you would naturally remain suspicious if I could not come up with some outstanding example of the use of detail from nonfiction as well. So I will. At the same time I want, though, to approach my example—helpfully, I hope—from a distance. So let me begin with a very intelligent question that students ask quite frequently: "About the concrete and specific—what if the nature of what you're writing about is general and abstract, as it is in philosophy?"

I think it's safe to admit by this time that on many an occasion the specific material in the four, five, or more sentences after the topic sentence will consist of specific *explanations* or be combined to present one specific *explanation.* Here is an example.

> *Being* cannot be defined. Yes, we all know what it is. In fact, that things exist was obviously our very first thought, our first realization, when our minds came to life (whenever that was). But knowing something and defining it are two different things. Defining means *limiting*—that is, cutting off the thing we define from everything else that is not *it.* So if we defined a vacuum cleaner simply as "a machine," people would say, "why, a car is a machine too, and so is a lawn mower. What *is* a vacuum cleaner? We go on, then, to say that a vacuum cleaner is a machine that uses an electric fan to produce suction at an opening that is passed over rugs, furniture, and so forth, to remove dust and dirt.
>
> In this way we have cut the vacuum cleaner off from every other machine, like a car or a lawn mower, with which it might otherwise be confused, and have *defined* it. But *being*—existence—cannot be cut off from *anything.* For one fact about *everything* is that it *exists,* has being: a vacuum cleaner, a car, a lawn mower, steel, wood, air, an atom, an electron—they all exist, all have being. So we cannot say that being is different from anything else, because the anything else will also have being. Or, if you say that we define by describing something in terms of its parts or its origin, why, pure being *has* no parts, has no origin (its origin would have to exist—have being—too, obviously). True, you could say "Being is existence" or "Being is the quality by which something *is.*" But *existence* and *is* are just different ways of saying *being;* they are synonyms; and synonyms do not really define, they just translate. Being, it is said, cannot be defined because it must enter into and transcend every definition.

Now admittedly that kind of paragraph is very far from "If Joe Greenberg didn't have to work thirty hours a week as a checker at the Spend-Easy Supermarket, he would have more time to study his chemistry and calculus. As it is, all day Sunday. . . ." The essential details of the paragraph on being—I mean the details we couldn't really leave out—are specific *explanations,* or arguments; and admittedly, though they are specific in their way, they still tend to be made up of abstract and general terms. And that is what I have used the paragraph as an example of.

But at the same time, you must have noticed that the paragraph does contain *examples.* And they are not there, you understand, just to make the paragraph more lively. For exactly where the vacuum cleaner is introduced as an example, the ordinary reader would have stopped being able to follow the line of argument. Thus the examples of the vacuum cleaner and the lawn mower and the car are used to help make the paragraph clear. Other concrete things are also introduced, you notice, and serve the same purpose. In fact, further examples both near the beginning and near the end of the paragraph would have been useful.

I did not intend to bring the following matter to your attention, but as long as it's right here in front of us we may as well deal with it. It's this: the paragraph we've just been talking about has also been made easier for the reader to read, follow, and understand because, despite talking about things, it also keeps mentioning *people.* The rule is that the more often you mention *people*—man, woman, child, postman, neighbor, student—and use pronouns referring to people *(I, my, me; we, our, us; you, your; he, his, him; she, her; they, their, them)*—the easier it is for readers to grasp the meaning of what you write.

Very well, our paragraph was in the highly general and abstract field of philosophy. And you see how we introduced concrete and fairly specific material into it. So to answer your question "What if the nature of what you're writing about is general and abstract?" I'd say that then you may have to use many abstract and general terms within your paragraph but that precisely because you're doing so, it's *especially* important to add concrete, specific examples or at least comparisons.

To illustrate what happens if you don't add concrete, specific examples, let me present the following paragraph, which, like the other, is in the field of philosphy.

> What is general does not exist formally outside our minds, where it is not independent of the particulars that it includes. But individuals that make up a genus or a species must have some common trait or traits actually in them to allow us reasonably to place them in their genus or species. Thus we can assert that though the general exists formally only in the mind, it exists fundamentally outside the mind. True, the mind can know only the general, and the senses only the particular, so that it might be argued that there is a permanent gap between the two. But the answer is that, in fact, it is neither the mind nor the senses that know, but the person, who knows by using both.

Well, there you are. How do you like it? Do you understand it? Or do you feel that you may understand the beginning, but begin to get lost as you go along and finally give up on it? Why? It's perfectly clear—in itself. *But it's not clear to you.* However, let me assure you that I could make it perfectly clear to you if you let me put in abundant *examples.*

But some of you won't let me, of course. You wanted an abstract and general paragraph on an abstract and general subject. Well, there it is; I hope you like it. Go ahead and write like that if you want to, without concrete examples. Most modern philosophers do. (They apparently write for one another; the greatest part of even the educated public can—or will—no more read what they write than they could read Aristotle in Greek.) So let those who reject Step 4 consider that last example. When they do succeed in reading it, they will find that its point furnishes a perfect proof from philosophy for Step 4.

I said "most modern philosophers," and that brings me at long last to the outstanding example of the use of Step 4 in nonfiction that you wanted. Now to make the example a particularly striking one, I'll take you to a book from the field of philosophy (which, as you have gathered, is the most general and abstract). The book I have chosen as an example is, in fact, the work of a modern philosopher: *Language in Thought and Action;* the author, S. I. Hayakawa (yes, the same Hayakawa who was in the headlines not so many years ago).[1]

Hayakawa's book actually deals with *semantics,* which today is considered to be in the field of philosophy. Now during the past quarter century quite a number of books have been written in that field. Some have sold well, some fairly well, some poorly—I'm sure unsold copies are yellowing in some basement to this day—but they all have been more or less forgotten. Young people, of course, have never heard of them. There is one exception: Hayakawa's book has gone on selling steadily for decades, has gone through I don't know how many printings, and, as I say, is being used as a textbook today.

What is the reason? Why has Hayakawa's book in its field achieved a success comparable to that of Ian Fleming's James Bond books in the field of the spy novel? Could it be that Hayakawa and Fleming have something in common? Apparently. For if there is any one thing that characterizes Hayakawa's *Language in Thought and Action,* it is the abundance of specific, concrete *examples,* the generous use of details. And I mean generous! Where another author would be content with one example, Hayakawa uses three, four, or five. Where another author would offer us a couple of details, Hayakawa sometimes gives us half a dozen or even a dozen. Never, that I recall, does he state an abstract or general proposition without turning at once to an example—or two, three, or five.

"But," you object (if you are anything like the students I know—and the objection is, again, an interesting one), "doesn't he use maybe *too many* examples? Too many specific, concrete details?"

Well—if I may be crass—I suspect Hayakawa's bank account would

[1] S. I. Hayakawa, *Language in Thought and Action,* 3rd ed. (New York: Harcourt Brace Jovanovich, 1972).

provide the answer to that objection. Few writers write books that sell (though the books may be highly meritorious and may be, for example, simply ahead of their time); Hayakawa did write one that sold and that continues to sell. It's pretty hard to argue with success, isn't it? Not that the sales by themselves prove anything about the worth of Hayakawa's book (that rests on other grounds), for many worthless books have sold very well while excellent ones have languished on the bookstore shelves. But the point is that certainly Hayakawa, writing on a *technical* subject, could not have had that many readers, year after year, if he hadn't some way of making difficult subject matter readable.

You'll be inclined to agree, I think, that his way is, or includes, the extraordinarily generous use of details and examples. If you'll go to the library, find Hayakawa's book, and open to almost any page, you'll find him doing exactly what I've been describing him as doing. If you have an instructor, perhaps he will choose to bring the book to class and read a number of short passages aloud. But since the details and anecdotes are so interesting, you'll have to remember not to get lost in the material, but to concentrate on what we are using the passages as examples of: generous use of specific, concrete details and abundant examples.

Remember the unsuccessful attempt at a paragraph on Keats that we read earlier? (See pages 45–46.) It was one example of writing that is *not* specific enough. Let's look at some other brief examples.

Charlemagne was a great king. He is celebrated in history and legend. He was of great aid to Christianity and to education during the Dark Ages.

Admittedly, this kind of writing may be partly a matter of scale and partly also a matter of your understanding of the material. If a student has only a minute or two to cover Charlemagne on a long test and can recall him only fairly well after a whole semester of history, a few of what the student thinks are the highlights of his reign are about all we can expect.

But if the student has more time and is expected to know more about Charlemagne, we must criticize his statements as generalizations. Why? First, "Charlemagne was a great king." So was Otto I; so was Louis IX; so was Frederick of Prussia. Were they all great in the same way? What does *great* mean in the student's statement? How was Charlemagne great? Next, "celebrated in history." May this not be said of a good many people? If *celebrated* means "praised by historians," what do they praise him for? If it means that they devote a good deal of space to him, how much? A whole chapter in a high school textbook covering the history of Europe? Next, "and legend." What legend, or legends? Any of importance? How about "of great aid to Christianity"? That might be said of hundreds of people. *How* did Charlemagne aid Christianity? Take "and to education." Alcuin, Thomas Aquinas, John Colet, Noah Webster, and Horace Mann all aided education; did Charlemagne do so in any of the same ways as they? Or would it be better to draw a parallel with King Alfred? Did Charlemagne's aid to education have anything to do with his aid to Christianity?

From this criticism you can gather that the generalities we condemn are statements so broad that though they are perhaps true, they are almost meaningless until we add some details; they are so broad that they describe not *this* case, but a thousand cases. It's as if someone (a native of the Brazilian jungles, I suppose) were to ask you, "What's television?" and you were to tell him, "Oh, it's a thing people have in their houses." That's true! But it's so general it's meaningless. For it's also true of a stove, a bed, a chair, a clock—the list is endless.

What we probably have to bring ourselves to see is that "My grandfather is neat," an assertion discussed earlier, is really not much better than "Television is a thing people have in their houses," because, standing alone, it's too general: I'm neat, you're neat; so is the next man—we tie our shoes, comb our hair, and do not carry unwrapped roast beef sandwiches in our pockets. What is *neat?*

True, we are allowed *in passing* to make fairly general remarks about people or things without going into detail, like "Brummel was a fastidious dresser," "Lincoln was homely," "My brother is a quiet fellow," "Miss Bauwens keeps records neatly." But the thing to note is that in these cases our listener or reader finds us specific enough; he gets the picture; questions do not come to his mind. If even in passing, though, we said "The speaker, who had an impairment, needed someone standing at his side on the platform," the listener or reader would immediately wonder "What was the impairment? Was he hard of hearing? Likely to fall? Terrified of crowds? What?"

From all this you can probably extract a rule. It calls, of course, for the exercise of good judgment, for it is this: you are to ask yourself, "Have I explained what I have said to my reader? Or do questions immediately come to his mind?" Decide what such questions would be if they did come to the reader's mind and supply sufficient details to answer them.

Assignment

Write a theme on a subject of your own choice for the purpose of being very critical of your use of sufficient detail. Impress on your mind as you write that in all the writing you do for the rest of your life you *must* remember the need for specific detail. It is all too easy to forget.

Let me tell you at the outset that Step 5 is going to cast new light on Step 2. More work? That's one way to look at it. Better themes? I think *that's* the way to look at it. Still another kind of thinking involved? Well, if it's a kind of thinking that other people are doing and we're not doing, hadn't we better find out about it? In fact, if we're not among the "fellows whom it hurts to think" that A. E. Housman speaks of, we ought to welcome the challenge of new problems of thinking. But the reconsideration of Step 2 will come up only in a later chapter, so at this point let's just consider Step 5 itself. It's simple.

STEP 5

Below the broken line, in the first sentence of the second paragraph and every paragraph following, insert a clear reference to the idea of the preceding paragraph.

102

Experience shows that both the meaning of some of the words and my use of them need explaining. So let's get that out of the way at once. First, the words: *preceding* means "which goes before"; *insert* means "put in"; *reference* means "mention," and here *reference to* means "mention and inclusion of." My use of *clear* may take some more explanation, but the time given to it will be worth it, because it's a key idea in both Step 5 and Step 6.

Clear as I've used it here is a synonym for *explicit*. *Explicit* means "spelled out, actually put into a word or words that a person can point to on the page." It is the opposite of *implicit* (or *implied*), which means "suggested, hinted at, or understood, but not actually put into words." An example will help you understand this. Suppose someone says to you, "Here it's 7 P.M. and I haven't had anything to eat all day." He's probably *implying* that he's hungry and would like something to eat, but he hasn't actually said so. He makes the fact that he's hungry or wants something to eat *explicit* only if he actually puts it into words: "Here it's 7 P.M., I haven't had anything to eat all day, and *I'm hungry.*"

Personally, I think some of the ills in our society would be remedied if people were willing to say just what they mean—when there's no reason not to, of course. If "I always have trouble moving this heavy table" means "Will you please move this table for me?" or "Will you please help me move this table?" why doesn't the speaker *say* "Will you please move this table for me?" or "Will you help me move this table?" It's not an indecent suggestion, after all, nor is it likely to make the speaker lose a friend. And it will save the speaker the customary grievance or anger over the fact that someone didn't take the hint—which in many cases the someone simply isn't alert enough at the moment to catch. I say this in the belief that many people resist Steps 1, 2, and 4 out of the feeling that for some reason it's not nice to come right out and say exactly what you mean. Admittedly, there are occasions when it would be very wrong to be blunt. But when there's no need for tact, why hesitate to express your point—definitely, specifically, explicitly? You want to be understood, don't you?

But to get back to Step 5. "Below the broken line" means below your first listing of sentences X, 1, 2, and 3 at the top of your page, under which you drew a broken line (see page 26). In other words, when I say "below the broken line" I mean where you begin the theme proper, where sentences X, 1, 2, and 3 are in their proper places in the theme.

"In the first sentence of your second paragraph and every paragraph following" means, obviously, in your sentences 2 and 3 (and others, if you have them) *in the theme proper.* Now I get a puzzling objection here; students say, "But you said earlier that under the broken line, sentences 1, 2, and 3 are to be copied down exactly as they are above the broken line." Yes, of course I did. But having reached a new step, we are now going to go further with what we have done; we are going to improve on it.

Now though Step 5, besides being simple, seems clear as day to me, I know it may not seem so to you. So what would I use to make it clear? Yes, that thing that *you* must always remember in order to make what *you* write clear—an example. Let's go back for an example to the anonymous theme on the need for a regular schedule of study. In that theme, above the dotted line, we find sentences X, 1, 2, and 3 as follows.

X A student must have a regular schedule of study.
1. Time must be set aside for study if there is going to be any time.

2. Often, only time to be filled provides the necessary spur to study.
3. Only time set aside will make study a serious profession.

All right, let's see what we should insert in (add to) sentences 2 and 3 according to Step 5. (We won't do anything to sentence 1—not yet, anyway.) Well, sentence 2 is to include now a mention of the idea in paragraph 1. What *is* the idea in paragraph 1? Although there's only one main idea in the paragraph, spelled out in the topic sentence, there's more than one way to look at it. First, sentence 1 says time must be set aside or there won't be any time. But what it says—and this is the second way of looking at it—is actually a *reason* for what is said in sentence X, isn't it?

Maybe you can think of still other ways of looking at sentence 1. In any case, if we look directly at what is the idea in paragraph 1, we may add to our sentence 2 to make it read this way (I'll put what I add in italics—slanting type—so you'll see clearly what we've done): "Often, only time *thus set aside and then needing* to be filled provides the necessary spur to study."

See? *Thus* here means "in this way," "in that way." In what way? In the way just talked about in the preceding paragraph, obviously. And so we've made an explicit reference to the idea in the preceding paragraph. Moreover, we've inserted the word *then.* The idea is this: the writer has said in sentence 1, "if there is going to be any time"; and the *then* in our revised sentence 2 means "then, when there *is* time." In other words, in sentence 1 the writer provides the time; *then* when we've got the time, we have to fill it.

Or, an easier—but weaker—way of doing the same thing is to make sentence 2 read: "Often only *that* time to be filled provides the necessary spur to study." *That time* can hardly mean anything but the time discussed in the previous paragraph, can it? So with just the word *that* we've made a clear reference to the preceding paragraph.

I should point out here that if you examine a number of essays or articles, you'll discover that over half (I'd guess) of the paragraphs you find will have *this, that, these* or *those* in the first sentence. You've never noticed that, have you? No, no more than you noticed that, say, over half of all paragraphs have or imply some equivalent of *for example* in the *second* sentence—something we've discussed already. The reason for *this, that, these,* and *those* in the first sentence of a paragraph is that it is a common way for writers to fulfill Step 5. Of course, you'll find if you look that all our six steps describe the way writing is actually done, as is plain to anyone who takes the trouble to notice *how* it's done. But we'll look at such examples later. Meanwhile, back to our discussion.

I was saying that we could also look at "Time must be set aside for study if there is going to be any time" as a *reason* for sentence X. In the same way we see that sentence 2 can be thought of as a reason for sentence 1. So we could revise our sentence 2 to read: "*Another reason for a regular schedule is that* often, only time to be filled provides the necessary spur to study."

Another reason can only indicate that we've already given *one* reason; otherwise *another* wouldn't make sense. But where did we give that first reason? In the first paragraph. So just by saying *another* we've made an explicit reference to the *idea* (in this case, we're viewing the idea as a reason) in the preceding paragraph.

Then right away we see that sentence 3 can be thought of as a reason, too; and that would take care of Step 5 in sentence 3: "*Still another reason is that* only time set aside will make study a serious profession."

The method we have just described—indicating that each paragraph provides a reason (or a cause, result, exception, objection, or qualification, as the case may be) *just as the preceding one did*—is a good, sufficient, and sometimes necessary way of observing the rule in Step 5, of linking paragraphs as it is called. But it is not the very best way. The best way, I think, is the way I showed you first.

But often there is still another way used: in the first sentence of a paragraph a writer often links paragraphs explicitly by saying *therefore* or *thus* or *for this reason* or *as a consequence* or *the result is that*—meaning that what he said in the preceding paragraph is the cause or reason that produces the result or consequence that he will be talking about in the new paragraph.

Sometimes the writer just begins the first sentence of the paragraph with *and,* which is an explicit sign (though sometimes a vague one) that tells us that the new paragraph is carrying on the same line of reasoning that we saw in the old.

I must stop to say that many of my students have told me that they've heard somewhere that it's wrong to begin a sentence with *and.* Since the little word *and* is so important a connective, I would like here and now to show the monstrous falseness of that rule. Let's take a look at the writing of Irving Howe, one of the more famous literary critics of our time—and an English professor too: "*And* something more would have to be said, as I am glad the Berkeley students did, about the pressures faced by state universities from boards of regents heavily weighted toward conservative and business ideologies and almost always without faculty or student representation."[1] And what when we look into Cardinal Newman, accounted the best English stylist of all time? "*And* this is the reason why it is more correct, as well as more usual, to speak of a University as a place of education than of instruction" (*Idea of a University,* Discourse V). Or in his *Apologia* (Chapter 3): "*And* thus I left the matter."

And it's not just professors who use *and* to begin their sentences. Let's look at the work of writers who live in and deal with the world outside the campus walls. Take James Baldwin: "*And* I'd known this avenue all my life, but it seemed to me again, as it had seemed on the day I'd first heard about Sonny's trouble, filled with a hidden menace which was its very breath of life." Or, "*And* thank God she was there, for I was filled with that icy dread again."[2] Or how about LeRoi Jones? "*And* it strikes me as monstrous that a nation or, for that matter, a civilization like our Western civilization, reared for the last five hundred years exclusively in the humanistic bombast of the Renaissance, should find it almost impossible to understand the strivings of enslaved peoples to free themselves."[3]

No, *and* is a very important connective, regularly used at the beginnings of sentences by our best writers. What you should remember out of what you have learned in the past about connectives is this, which *is* a sound general rule: do not use *also, however,* or *therefore* at the beginning of a sentence or a clause (see page 140).

Or, instead of *and* or similar expressions like *moreover* and *likewise,* the writer may use *but. But* indicates that the writer has presented something as true, and that you might therefore think a certain other thing is also true, whereas it is actually not. Thus we say, "It's raining today. *But* I'm going swimming anyway." Or "You can bisect an angle with a compass and a ruler. *But* you can't trisect one that way." Or "Financiers expected Giannini to oppose Franklin Delano Roosevelt's

[1] Irving Howe, *Steady Work: Essays in the Politics of Democratic Radicalism, 1953–1966* (New York: Harcourt Brace Jovanovich, 1966), p. 83.
[2] James Baldwin, "Sonny's Blues," from *Going to Meet the Man* (New York: Dial Press, 1965), reprinted in *Afro-American Literature: An Introduction,* edited by Robert Hayden, David J. Burrows, and Frederick R. Lapides (New York: Harcourt Brace Jovanovich, 1971), pp. 76, 77.
[3] LeRoi Jones, "Tokenism: 300 Years for Five Cents," from *Home: Social Essays* (New York: William Morrow, 1966), reprinted in *Another View: To Be Black in America,* edited by Gerald Messner (New York: Harcourt Brace Jovanovich, 1970), p. 259.

election. *But* he came out in favor of it." Or, of course, the writer may use some equivalent of *but* by inserting a word like *however, nevertheless,* or *still* into his sentence.

A special case is a linking or connective expression like *true, I grant, I admit, of course, naturally,* or *admittedly.* These expressions mean that in the new paragraph the writer is about to grant the truth of some facts that are, or seem to be, *against* the point he is making. They must eventually be followed, in the same paragraph or the next, by the word *but* (or its equivalent), followed in turn by an explanation of why they do not make the writer's point untrue.

For example, you may be arguing against the reelection of Q. T. Cicero as mayor of your town. *"True,"* you admit, "without a rise in taxes, he succeeded in creating lovely new municipal parks and in adding sidewalks to all our streets." Now you can't stop there, or it will look as if you've changed your mind about Q. T. Cicero—that he's not a bad guy but a good guy! So you have to go on and say *"But"* and then something like "what good are parks if you can't sit in them without being blackjacked, or sidewalks if you can't walk on them without being mugged, as happens every day under Q. T. Cicero's administration?"

The need for a word like *true* before arguments or facts opposed to your point—always eventually followed by *but* and an explanation of why those facts or claims do not demolish your point—is sometimes overlooked. And the result is utter confusion for the reader!

Let's look now at a few more examples of Step 5. Charles Dickens in *Hard Times* (Chapter 5) talks about Coketown as a town of monotonous appearance, sounds, and habits, and then begins the next paragraph with *"These attributes* of Coketown"—meaning, of course, the qualities of the town he has just mentioned in the preceding paragraph.

Charles Darwin talks about his book *The Origin of Species;* he begins his next paragraph with "The main conclusion arrived at in *this work,"* meaning by *this work* his book *The Origin of Species,* which he has just been discussing in the previous paragraph (*The Descent of Man,* Chapter 21).

In an article in the *Edinburgh Review* (1830) Thomas Macaulay summarizes in one paragraph Robert Southey's views of the manufacturing system, then begins the next paragraph, "Mr. Southey does not bring forward a single fact in support of *these views."*

But I'm doing your work for you. Let's let you get on with your assignment.

Assignment

Go to an article or two of your choice (but not a news story in a newspaper) and examine the beginnings of the paragraphs. Prove to yourself that the writer has followed Step 5, and notice the various ways he has done it.

NEW INSIGHTS

If we are going to hook the first sentence of each paragraph to the preceding paragraph, as explained in the last chapter, then those paragraphs must already be related in some way. To take some easy illustrations first, suppose you wrote for sentences 1, 2, and 3 (as I know you wouldn't) that a certain person always wears brown suits, plays tennis, and is a Democrat. How would you ever connect paragraphs about those three statements? You could only do so artificially by saying something like "Besides wearing brown suits, he plays tennis." But nobody would be fooled into thinking that you had really established any connection between the two ideas. Yet, a warning: students do try to fake connections in that way. Don't you do it!

But let's take a slightly harder—but still real—example. Say someone's sentences X, 1, 2, and 3 are the following.

X Nikola Tesla was a remarkable inventor.

110

1. He could correctly visualize in his head the most complicated electrical apparatus in exact detail.
2. It was he who successfully put Faraday's alternating current to work in the polyphase power system we all use today.
3. He also discovered an unlimited source of electrical power, transmissible over any distance without wires and almost without loss of power.

Now how are you going to connect sentences 1, 2, and 3? Sentences 2 and 3 are easy: both tell us of revolutionary inventions in the field of electronics, the one invention now used universally because of the failures and breakdowns that accompanied Edison's old direct-current system, and other never used because of the impossibility of monopolistic control of it.

But what about connecting those two sentences to paragraph 1? Aren't we back to the brown suits, tennis, and membership in the

Democratic party? True, the extraordinary ability to visualize complicated apparatus in practical detail may well have helped to make Tesla
a remarkable inventor. And his two great inventions, the polyphase
power system and the unlimited source of electrical power, are obviously connected with "was a remarkable inventor," too.

But the trouble is that though sentence 1 as well as sentences 2 and 3
are all connected with sentence X, they are connected with it in such
different ways that there is no connection between sentence 1 and the
other two. It is as if you said, "This orange weighs two ounces, is soft,
and contains potassium." All three statements are true of the orange;
but they are such different truths that they just don't belong together.
One has to do with weight, another with consistency, and still another
with chemical content, which have in turn nothing to do with one
another.

So in our example, sentence 1 has to do with a quality of Tesla's
mind and imagination, and sentences 2 and 3 have to do with another
kind of thing entirely—that is, two electronic systems that he invented.
Thus sentence 1 and the other two sentences just don't belong together.

I know that an objection has been forming in your mind. You say,
"On the contrary, I can see how sentence 1 *is* connected with sentences 2 and 3. For it was Tesla's almost unique ability to visualize
things (sentence 1) that enabled him to produce those revolutionary
inventions (sentences 2 and 3)." That's a good objection, and you
seem to have arrived at a solution to our problem. (Whether you have
or not, readers will at least be more comfortable with "As a result of
this almost unique power of visualization, he was able to invent . . ."
than they would be with such *obviously* false connections as "Besides
wearing brown suits, he also played tennis"—where despite the word
besides you have shown no connection in the world between brown
suits and tennis.)

But I'm afraid that even with *as a result of,* we're still in trouble. For I
have still another question: is the *theme* about Tesla's powers of
visualization? Or is it about two of his inventions? It can't be about
both; they're different subjects. Oh, I can see that if it were about
Tesla's powers of visualization, you'd naturally *bring in* the inventions; but you'd keep it clear to the reader that the inventions were
there strictly to illustrate Tesla's ability to visualize, and that the theme
hadn't turned into something about *them.* That is, they would be
clearly *subordinated,* as we say, to the main topic; you wouldn't make

independent statements about them. (By the way, for a good treatment, with exercises, of keeping to the *point* in main clauses while enriching a paragraph with additional information, but confining that information to *subordinate* constructions—adjectives, adverbs, prepositional phrases, participial and gerund phrases, relative clauses and subordinate clauses—see Gallo and Rink's *Shaping College Writing*.[1])

Or conversely, if the theme were about Tesla's inventions, I can see how you'd *bring in* his power to visualize, but not give it a paragraph of its own. It would be clearly subordinated to the main subject (the inventions).

Perhaps it will help you to see this point if you notice that despite all the talking I've been doing about Tesla, this chapter hasn't turned into a chapter about Tesla. For everything I've said about him has been clearly for the sake of illustrating my point: namely, that in a theme the paragraphs all have to be connected among themselves, as well as with the theme sentence, and that to be so connected they must all be the result of taking the theme sentence *in the same sense: remarkable inventor* can't mean "having remarkable mental powers" at one moment and "producing revolutionary inventions" at the next. It must mean the same thing throughout your theme.

But I think we can get to the root of all this if we ask ourselves, "How did the writer of the theme on Tesla get into this trouble in the first place?" And I believe that the answer is that he was too hasty and careless in writing his sentence X. We've got to face the fact that sentence X is not just something that pops out of our heads and that we hasten to get down on paper so we go on to sentences 1, 2, and 3. *It is the whole theme*—reduced, of course, to one sentence. It is our whole point, our one idea. So much are we inclined to forget this that I'll take it up again in the next chapter, along with some helpful related material.

First of all, the writer made the assertion that as an inventor Tesla was remarkable. Now *remarkable* is one of those words that do not convey definite information about anything, but simply praise or condemn it. Other such words are *good, bad, fine, poor, wonderful, marvelous, disappointing, interesting, dull,* and of course *fantastic* and *fabulous, terrible* and *awful.*

It's easy to assert that surfing or skiing or my aunt Minnie is fantastic,

[1]Joseph D. Gallo and Henry W. Rink, *Shaping College Writing: Paragraph and Essay,* 2nd ed. (New York: Harcourt Brace Jovanovich, 1973), pp. 35–39, 61–63.

that Greek is dull, or that a book is interesting. But where will you get the sentences 1, 2, and 3 that will *show* those things? How am I going to prove that chess is wonderful? Oh yes, I can make assertions of various kinds about it; but will those assertions really add up to the fact that it's wonderful—really make a reader, too, feel that it's wonderful?

Given adequate facts about Tesla—a rare genius indeed, whose inventions are found in the homes of every one of us—the reader might very well be persuaded that he's remarkable. But the second trouble with *remarkable* and other words like those just listed is that they also often say too much. What is advertised as a remarkable new dish-washing detergent turns out to be satisfactory. It washes dishes. But it doesn't dry them and put them away! We may as well call every student who gets an *A* in mathematics a genius, or everyone who has a thousand dollars in the bank rich. So not only is it difficult to *show* that *anything* is, say, fascinating; it is also assuming too heavy a debt to promise to show most things as fascinating when they are, in sober truth, fairly commonplace after all.

But the real trouble with words like *marvelous, interesting, wonderful, dull,* and *disappointing* is that they describe not the thing you seem to be talking about, but someone's (perhaps your own) *reactions* to that thing. The result is that if my sentence X is "My aunt Minnie is fascinating," I should logically tell whom she fascinates—for example, "My aunt Minnie fascinates me." Then my sentences 1, 2, and 3 should really be not directly about Aunt Minnie, but about my reactions to her.

Finally, *remarkable inventor* is like *great king,* which we saw was so broad as to be almost meaningless. Isn't there a hat that will fit Tesla a little more closely, and not fit so many other people? Wouldn't it at least be more informative to say that Tesla was a *revolutionary* inventor? (His alternating-current polyphase system *revolutionized* all our use of electricity, and his wireless transmission of power might have done so.)

Practically, I believe that if the writer of the sentences X, 1, 2, and 3 on Tesla had avoided the trap of *remarkable,* he would have had a series 1, 2, and 3 that was actually connected and that he could have shown was connected in the first sentences of paragraphs 2 and 3.

Since we're speaking of *showing connections,* I'm going to deal with two related matters here. First, I'm sometimes asked whether we can't put *above the dotted line* the connective material called for in Step 5. Then sentences X, 1, 2, and 3 above the dotted line could be used in the theme proper, as the introductory paragraph.

My answer is threefold. First, wait until you're writing the theme proper to use Step 5, because knowing how one paragraph ends will help you swing gracefully with your connective material into the new one. Second, after you've finished your theme, you can transfer the connective material up to the sentences above the dotted line, if you have some purpose in doing so. Third, a combination of sentences X, 1, 2, and 3 and their connectives as an introduction would be both disproportionate and confusing; disproportionate, because roughly a whole fourth or fifth of your theme would be introduction, and confusing, because you would, as a result of it, repeat some material so soon that the reader would say: "Didn't he just say that? Or have I lost my place? Yes, he did; what's he repeating it for?"

In a much longer theme, however, you might well add to sentence X a summary of the points the paragraphs are going to cover. Thus, "The conquistadors found in Mexico an Indian civilization surpassing the European civilization in certain regards—notably in the construction of cities, the estimation of the movements of the stars, and the production of hybrid grain." Then the writer would go on with a sentence 1 saying that the Mexicans were able to build the largest cities in the world at that time (the sixteenth century), followed by a very long paragraph (perhaps broken up by indentations).

Then the writer would indicate in sentence 2 that the Mexican calendar, more accurate than the European, showed superior knowledge of astronomy, and he would go into considerable detail about that. Finally, he would write that the Indians, by hybridization, or artificial selection, had produced what is now the staple feed crop in North America—corn—and then go on to discuss that. But this leads me to my next point.

The second matter related to showing connections is this: a friend of mine advises the use of a summary of the kind I've just described *with each topic sentence.*[2] That is, the kind of topic sentence he advises will first state the point of the paragraph and then indicate briefly the line of development the paragraph will take. I'll show you an example of such a topic sentence, with its paragraph, and I'll put the added material in the topic sentence in italics.

Social justice seems the only protection against communism, *for where it exists communism cannot prevail, but where it is absent many see communism as inevitable.* A certain minimal social justice, that

[2]William F. Smith and Raymond D. Liedlich, *From Thought to Theme,* 4th ed. (New York: Harcourt Brace Jovanovich, 1974), pp. 5–6.

provides the majority of workers and tillers of the soil with something definitely more to lose "than their chains," leaves most of the common people with no incentive for radical change. Such is the situation in most places in the United States, except for the inner-city ghettos, the camps of the migrant laborers, and the backwoods homes of the mountain people and the rural poor. The majority of the people in America have their beer and baseball, their television and annual paid vacation, their health insurance and Social Security, a full stomach, clothes on their back, shoes on their feet, and grade school and high school for their children; the underprivileged in the United States are the minority—albeit a large minority, too large a minority. But how different is the situation in some parts of Latin America, where hunger, bare feet, and tattered clothes are the rule, where most people live in hovels, in swarming tenements, or in the streets, where illiteracy is widespread, where illness goes untreated, and where most people live without hope. There is where communism, which at least promises something better and at the most could hardly be worse, can gain a foothold. And it may; some of our American presidents have spoken hardly veiled warnings of this. Until the people are given something more to lose than their chains, until they can see a minimum of social justice established, there and in other countries where the people have nothing, the threat of communism is imminent. No amount of propaganda, no amount of gunfire will stop it. Social justice, in contrast, will render it powerless.

Though I think I could criticize that paragraph on several grounds, it does illustrate, I think, the device of adding to the topic sentence a clue to what line the paragraph will take. It also demonstrates what a useful device that addition to the topic sentence is: it keeps the writer thinking of what he is going to say before he says it, and it guides the reader to a quicker, surer understanding. Moreover, knowing ahead of time what the paragraph is to be like, the reader has the comfortable feeling that the paragraph, when he comes to it, is as it should be.

While I don't insist that you use that device at this point in your career, I obviously recommend it. Let me point out at the same time two things: first, this device is more useful in long paragraphs than in short ones; second, while you are using it you must not forget Step 5—namely, to make a clear reference to the preceding paragraph in the second and following topic sentences.

Assignment

On a carefully selected sentence X of your own choice write a series 1, 2, and 3 that are connected not only with sentence X but among themselves. Write a theme—incorporating, as usual, these sentences X, 1, 2, and 3—giving careful attention to Step 5. If you want, also add to the topic sentences of the paragraphs a brief indication of how they will be developed, a device we just saw illustrated at the end of this chapter.

A USEFUL REVIEW

Since Step 1 is of central importance in the whole matter of composition as well as of central importance in any individual theme, it may be good at this point not only to reemphasize its importance and caution you to give it your most careful consideration but to suggest by way of review that you apply to any sentence X three tests.

First, is this sentence X the *point* of my theme? Is this the point that I'm really seeking to make? If you are asked to write a theme on some teacher you have had and choose as your sentence X "Miss López was my geometry teacher," you must ask yourself if that is what you want as the *point* of your whole paper. Certainly it is not. At best it is an introduction or a beginning or a title; and you should get it out of your head that sentence X is a beginning sentence or a title.

Second—getting at the same thing from another point of view—is this sentence X what I really intend to write about? Suppose you choose as your sentence X "*Cinderella* is an interesting story." Do you really intend to discuss the sources of interest in the story—or something else? The sources of interest, probably, are a central character

118

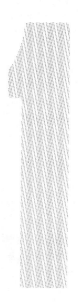

suffering injustice (at the hands of her stepmother and stepsisters), the reader's various fears for her (principally that she will fail to win the prince), a culminating revelation (through the slipper fitting), and a reversal of situation. Are these what you actually plan to discuss? Or is your sentence X merely a way to introduce the topic *Cinderella,* whereupon you simply retell the story?

Third, getting at the same thing from still another point of view, pretend that your sentence X is an answer to a question. To what question is, for instance, "Miss López was my geometry teacher" an answer? Is it an answer to "Who was your geometry teacher?" or "What did Miss López teach you?" Is that what you are imagining your reader wants to know? No, you are probably imagining he wants to know "What was Miss López like?" So your answer—your sentence X—must sum up what sort of teacher she was: "Miss López made complicated things seem clear"; "Miss López made us think"; "Miss López was conscientious."

This third test becomes more important when a question has actually been asked or implied. And to guarantee to yourself that you are answering the question asked (or implied) and not some *other* question, you must learn and apply these additional rules: first, *answer specifically the interrogative words (question words) in the question.* If the question is "Where is the richest soil in Iowa?" you must answer the question word *where,* and thus your answer must be a *place* (since, you know, *where* means "what place"). If the interrogative is *who,* your immediate answer must be a person; if it is *why,* your immediate answer must be a reason (and will no doubt contain the word *because*). Note that your answer is a sentence X, oral or written, and that you can, after giving it, go on to elaborate on it either briefly or at length, as the circumstances dictate. Or, of course, if the question is one that can be answered yes or no, answer it immediately, yes or no. "Is there character development in *Cinderella?*" Then add your explanation. Do not begin with the explanation; begin with the answer, which is your sentence X.

Second, as far as possible, *use in the answer the same words as in the question.* Thus "Where is the richest soil in Iowa?" *"The richest soil in Iowa is* in the northwest quarter of the state." (The answer does need some qualifications, I admit; but give the qualifications *later,* and do not use them as an introduction to your answer. Instead, answer the question immediately, using—as I just said—as far as possible the same words as in the question.) Similarly, "How does the glass slipper function in the story?" *"The glass slipper functions in the story* as the instrument of the central revelation." (And notice that *as* goes naturally with the interrogative word *how.*)

In brief, you must create an answer that fits the question as perfectly as Cinderella's foot fitted the glass slipper. Doing so gives you a perfect sentence X.

In the beginning of this chapter I asked if your intention in writing sentence X was to retell the story of a subject assigned for a theme. For students who plan to go on to other English classes, in which they will have to write papers on stories, novels, plays, or poems, it is of the utmost importance to learn still another rule: *in your theme, unless you are expressly instructed to do so, do not retell the story.* That is, do not give the plot; do not tell what happened.

The reasons for this rule are not difficult to understand. First, since the author has told the story once, it is utterly pointless for you to tell it again. Second, in your theme it is up to you not to tell the story (which has already been told), but to talk *about* the story, which is a very different thing. Unlike your history or psychology professor, your English professor will not consider memorization the most important part of your studying. He will be more interested in your interpretation of what you have read. Third (though actually this is the same reason as the one preceding), except in a creative writing class, you are supposed to be writing exposition, not description or narration, and a summary of what happened in a story is narration pure and simple.

No, you must use of what happened only what you *must* use. If you assert that chance intervenes at several points in *Cinderella,* you will want to specify at what points: when the prince gives a ball and when Cinderella leaves one slipper behind. You tell only enough of what happened to support your assertion.

If you cannot cure yourself of the fatal malady of summarizing the plot, do this: *pretend* that at the beginning of your theme you have written a whole page or more in which you have told all that happened in the story, novel, play, or poem. Then begin your actual writing *after that,* discussing character, theme, imagery, or whatever you have chosen or been instructed to write on.

Assignment

Make up a series of easy questions followed by answers that include as far as possible the same words as the question: "What is your name?" "*My name is* Robert Kenyon." "Is Borneo in Africa?" "No, *Borneo is not in Africa.*"

Then make up a series of sentence X's, each followed by a series 1, 2, and 3, in which sentence X is an answer to a question: "Why should we pay taxes to support education?" "*We should pay taxes to support education* because the education of others eventually benefits us." Take care that sentences 1, 2, and 3 are connected not only with sentence X, but among themselves, as explained in the preceding chapter.

Step 6 is really the logical forerunner of Step 5. But I've put it in sixth place for reasons I won't delay you by explaining; I think you'll see for yourself. Anyway, let me approach Step 6 in this way: you remember that you learned somewhere, perhaps as far back as grade school, that every sentence must—what? Every sentence must express a complete thought, wasn't that it? (That every sentence must have a subject and a predicate is really another way of saying the same thing, for only a statement that somebody or something is or was, does or did something is a thought.)

Today you are going to learn a second thing that every sentence must do; and that is the matter of Step 6.

STEP 6

Make sure every sentence in your theme is connected with, and makes a clear reference to, the preceding sentence.

122

That statement stuns some people. It seems to them to claim to be a truth—a big truth—about all writing; yet since they have never heard it before, how can it be true?

In fact, I had teaching with me once, as a practice teacher, an intelligent young woman who was doing graduate work in English at one of our state universities. She had previously been a technical editor in the aerospace industry. She enjoyed her work teaching Steps 1 through 5 and did it excellently, I am happy to say. I suspect Step 5 may have been something of an eye opener for her; but when I proposed Step 6 to her, she looked at me as if I were out of my mind. "Why, that's simply not so," she said.

"Well," I said, "don't take my word for it. But go to any printed essay or article that you think is well written, and see whether every sentence in it doesn't connect with, and make clear reference to, the preceding sentence."

She went away shaking her head, her eyes clouded with doubt. But a couple of days later she returned, after having done some conscientious and extensive investigation, and said simply, "Now I see why I haven't been getting A's on my papers at the university."

Before making further comment, however, I must turn to Step 6 itself. First, what does *connected with* mean? It means that the idea of any sentence must be an idea about the sentence just before it. An example will make this clear: "Henry Ford, in the belief that in order to buy American products, workers had to have the money to pay for them, raised his automotive workers' wages to five dollars a day. At first, this unprecedented raise for workers shocked and angered many other manufacturers throughout the country."

There you have two sentences coming one after the other somewhere in the course of some paragraph in an article. This coming one after another, of course, is the situation that Step 6 is talking about. Now the first point is that the second sentence of this pair (of *any* pair) must be about the first of the pair. Is it, in this case?

Why, yes! What shocked and angered some manufacturers in the second sentence was the decision to raise wages that the first sentence is about. This, then, is what we mean when we say that the second sentence is connected in thought with the first.

I hope I make myself clear when I speak of two sentences. I mean *any* two sentences coming one after another. In other words, take your pencil and put it at random on any sentence in any book; we'll call that sentence 2. Now move your eyes to the sentence just before the one you have your pencil on; that sentence before the one you have your pencil on we'll call sentence 1. Now sentence 2 has to be about sentence 1; it 's as simple as that. What you see is that any sentence anywhere has to be about the one just before it.

Let me caution you that in the kind of analysis you have just made, you should always move backwards, from sentence 2 to sentence 1. (I won't take up your time by explaining why.) If you want to, you can *then* go forward from sentence 1 to sentence 2 in the same pair of sentences, seeing how sentence 1 receives further development in sentence 2.

At this point you can, if you wish, put down this book and make a brief investigation of any two sentences in an essay or article of your choice, seeing how those sentences illustrate Step 6.

So much for the first part of Step 6. For the second part, we can, to start with, use the same example we used for the first part. And the second part should be easy, because you're already acquainted, from Step 5, with the idea of a clear reference. Let's see: "Henry Ford, in the belief that in order to buy American products, workers had to have the money to pay for them, raised his automotive workers' wages to five dollars a day. At first, this unprecedented raise for workers shocked and angered many other manufacturers throughout the country."

Now what words can we actually point to in the second sentence that refer to the first sentence—match some word or words in it that we can also point to? Well, there is "raise" in sentence 2, which goes with "raised . . . wages" and "to five dollars a day" in sentence 1; to five dollars a day is, in fact, what the raise was. What about "other manufacturers"? Well, *manufacturers* goes with "Ford," who was—and is being presented as—a manufacturer; and *other* not only implies but actually means that there is at least one manufacturer mentioned elsewhere—the one in this case being Ford. (This is the relationship of contrast, made explicit—clear—by the use of *other,* which we'll talk more about in a moment.)

Thus you have seen analyzed two sentences that occur together, the second both meaning something about the first and referring to it in actual words. That is the essence of the matter. But before I conclude this chapter, I must explain *clear reference* more systematically. First, you remember that *clear* here means "explicit" or "spelled out"; what is explicit you can actually point to, with your pencil, on the page. But what forms, you may ask, can explicit reference take? The following forms are the principal ones (and as you study them, all of Step 6 will become clearer to you).

FORMS OF EXPLICIT REFERENCE

First, *repeat in sentence 2 (the second of any two sentences) a word used in sentence 1 (the first of those two sentences).* For instance, "Educated in classical culture, and a passionate admirer of antiquity, *Gerbert* gave the young Otto III a lively sense of the majesty of the Roman Empire and a desire to revive it. In 999 *Gerbert* himself became pope." Here, the *Gerbert* of sentence 2 repeats the *Gerbert* of sentence 1.

Second, *use in sentence 2 a synonym of a word in sentence 1.* We use *synonym* here in the broad sense of any word or words that designate in sentence 2 the same person or thing mentioned in sentence 1. For instance, "The *abacus* was used as a calculator in the Tigris-Euphrates Valley five thousand years ago. The *device* is still used in Japan today." Here *device* is used as a synonym for *abacus.* (There are some other forms of explicit reference here, but we'll let them go for the moment.)

Third, *use in sentence 2 an antonym of a word in sentence 1.*
Antonym means a word designating the opposite of something. For
our purposes, we can extend its meaning to include anything used in
contrast to something or anything clearly used to show a *difference*
between two things. For example: "Ecuador is *hot.* Antarctica is *cold.*"
Here *cold* in sentence 2 is a clear antonym of *hot.* (The more easily the
reader can recognize two words as opposites, the clearer the connection between the two sentences will be. But the use of such obvious
antonyms is not always possible.) But not only is *cold* an antonym of
hot; we also see that Antarctica is presented as an opposite of
Ecuador, or at least as something significantly different from Ecuador.
Do you see that? It's important that you do.

Another example: "The world, of course, is approximately *round.*
But the surveyor, for his purposes, pretends that the world is *flat.*"
Here *flat* in sentence 2 is obviously an antonym for *round.* You notice
that *the world* stays the same, so to speak (while *round* changes to
flat): it is repeated in sentence 2 from sentence 1. But a sharp student
will notice that *the surveyor, for his purposes* forms a kind of opposite
to *of course* and that *pretends* is clearly an opposite of *is.*

Another example: "In Southern California, *wall-to-wall carpeting* is
almost universal. Even in the houses of the wealthy, *Oriental rugs* are
rarely seen." What is being contrasted here? Though we can't say that
Oriental rugs and *wall-to-wall carpeting* are *antonyms* in the strict
sense, or even that they are *opposites,* in this pair of sentences they are
being *used* as antonyms; that is, they are clearly being contrasted. (If
the particular reader or readers the writer has in mind wouldn't sufficiently understand the contrast, the writer would naturally have to
explain at greater length.) *Rarely seen* is, of course, an opposite of
universal.

Fourth, *use a pronoun in sentence 2 to refer to an antecedent in
sentence 1.* Pronouns, for our purposes here, are the words *he, his,
him; she, her; it, its; they, their, them; this, that; these, those; some;
any; another, others; none; all.* Antecedents are the persons or things
that pronouns refer to. For instance, "*Early American settlers* did not
drink tea or coffee at breakfast. *They* drank beer instead." Here *they* (a
pronoun) obviously means "early American settlers" (which we therefore call the antecedent of *they*). You will notice that this form of
explicit, or clear, reference is very common indeed, and that a pronoun
acts pretty much like a synonym.

Fifth, *use in sentence 2 a word commonly paired with a word in
sentence 1.* What do I mean by *commonly paired?* Well, *pen* and *ink*

are examples; so are *brush* and *paint.* There are perhaps thousands of others, and sometimes the group includes more than a pair: *reader-writer; hub-spokes-rim; seeing-hearing; bacon-eggs; knife-fork-spoon; container-contents; time-clock; actor-audience-stage-theater-play.* Mind you, they must be things so commonly thought of together that the reader makes the connection automatically.

Sixth, *repeat a sentence structure.* This may be the hardest form for you to understand, but you needn't worry, because it is the one used least often. Here is an example: "The air was stilled. The sky grew blacker. The leaves turned their silver side up. The thunder muttered." Here, of course, the writer is suggesting that each statement is connected with the others because each is part of the same phenomenon—the coming of a Midwestern storm. And he signals this connection to the reader by repeating the word *the,* then giving the subject and then the predicate. He strengthens the signal by making his sentences approximately the same length.

I give you this form of explicit reference not because you will use it much and not even because I simply want to be complete, but because it is the real reason behind the rule that you should vary the length of your sentences and not always begin them with the subject. For the real reason for that rule is that if we repeat a sentence pattern—for instance, short sentences with the subject first—the reader will at least unconsciously feel that we are indicating that there is also a pattern in the meaning. He will feel that our sentences are meant to be parallel, that they form some kind of series so that we could (if we wanted to) label the sentences *1, 2, 3, 4* or *a, b, c, d.*

If showing parallel meanings weren't our real intention, the reader would be misled, and our failure to vary the lengths and beginnings of sentences would interfere with *clarity.* (Readers of this book who are acquainted with formal rhetoric should notice that variety and euphony add grace to a composition, but that their fundamental contribution—just like that of unity, coherence, and emphasis—is *clarity.*) But by the same token, do not make the opposite mistake: *do* express similar thoughts in the same form, so that the reader grasps at once their similarity: "He was crafty. He was self-seeking. He was dishonest."

Seventh, *use a connective in sentence 2 to refer to an idea in sentence 1.* This form of explicit reference, one of very great importance, is discussed at length later in this book. It is enough to say now that such connectives are words and expressions like *for, therefore, as a result, for example, however, and,* and *but.*

For instance, "I cannot lend you my pen. *For* if I do, I won't have anything to take notes with in biology class." Or, "I learn that about 1050 Leo IX received the king of Scotland, Macbeth, who had come to Rome to seek pardon for his crimes. I must, *therefore,* revise my thinking about the historical background of Shakespeare's play *Macbeth.*" Or, "The postal clerk asked Sullivan for identification. *But* Sullivan declared that he had left his billfold, containing his various proofs of identification, on his yacht."

In connection with this seventh form of explicit reference, let me emphasize that most writers do not use it often enough. If you want to increase your word power, do not spend your time memorizing words commonly given you to enrich your vocabulary, like *sciolist, lachrymose, bravura, fiduciary,* and *piscivorous;* you may never have a use for them. Spend your time instead learning the meanings of, experimenting with, and *using as often as possible* both the little words we use to *connect* sentences and the little words we use to show connections *within* sentences *(because, as, as if, although, if, whereas).* And pay special attention to them when you are reading. In short, concentrate on *them,* for it is those words that will give you word power—in reading, writing, and thinking.)

In any case, whatever you write must stand up to this test: does every sentence not only refer to the idea of the preceding sentence, but also make an *explicit* (clear) reference to it?

Finally, when you are writing explicit references it's important that you control the placement of them, since your readers will understand you more quickly and easily when your linking word or words are put at or near the beginning of the new sentence. Leaving the linking word or phrase till later results in sentence pairs like this: "I *left out the minus sign* before my answer. The instructor counted my whole answer wrong because of *that one little mistake.*" Here *that one little mistake* in the second sentence provides the link, for it refers to *left out the minus sign* in the first sentence. Now by bringing *that one little mistake* nearer to the beginning of the second sentence, we get the following smoother, more quickly understood transition: "I *left out the minus sign* before my answer. Because of *that one little mistake* the instructor counted my whole answer wrong." But note: when you are using the seventh form of explicit reference, you will have to be careful with words like *however,* which should not come at the very beginning of the sentence (see page 140).

As a quick mental exercise in putting the explicit reference as near as possible to the beginning of the sentence, check back through the examples of explicit reference given so far in this chapter to see whether or not you can bring the explicit reference in each pair of sentences nearer to the beginning of the second sentence.

Now if you want the shortest writing program possible, you can conclude the book right here (unless your instructor objects, of course). If you are concluding here, let me suggest as a final assignment that you go slowly through the themes you have written so far, checking to see whether every sentence does refer to—and does make an explicit reference to—the sentence before it. You will find that in almost every case you have observed Step 6 without thinking about it! For the future, however, you will have to check each sentence as you write it. For so far you have written about things familiar to you. When you have to write about *other* people's ideas—the Constitution, the Romantic movement, psychosis, or erosion—*then* is when you run the danger of writing sentences that don't really join; and this you simply must not do. "The moon revolves around the earth. Like the earth, it is a solid body and roughly spherical." Are those two consecutive sentences really connected in idea? No. That kind of lack of connection is what you must train yourself to avoid.

The reason I think you may want to stop with that assignment and not go on with the next chapter is that the next chapter seems not only to be taken up with fine points and theory, but to be interrupted with matters connected only accidentally with Step 6. Let me assure you that what seem fine points and theory are in fact practical remedies I have devised for common faults that I meet—and for years have met—from day to day in students' themes. Dry and drawn-out my material may seem, yet it is immediately practical. Some of this practical material is only half-connected with Step 6, I agree; but I think it is useful for students to know. Yet I can see that, in view of the difficulties, some of us may part company at this point.

But we're parting friends, because I know—and, more important, *you* know—that *you can now write a theme*. If you've done your reasonable best to follow my instructions so far, your papers will always have a clear point, be clearly connected throughout, and contain not thin repetition, but meaningful details and examples. As one student, when he reached this point in my book, enthusiastically exclaimed, "I can *write!* I didn't think I ever could."

STEP FURTHER INSIGHTS

Those of us who are going on to the end of the book can now look more closely at certain aspects of Step 6; and since there is no certain order in which those aspects must be taken up, perhaps we can look first at a couple of exceptions.

Students, by the way, seem to love exceptions. Perhaps they think that if a rule has exceptions, it can't be much of a rule, and that therefore they needn't bother their heads much about it. In any case, this is a good place to give two warnings: first, never try to base a rule on exceptions; second, become thoroughly at home with a rule before interesting yourself in the exceptions. So with Step 6.

But already in Step 5 we have met a possible exception to Step 6: the first sentence of a paragraph is to refer to the idea in the preceding paragraph, rather than to the idea in the preceding sentence (which is, of course, the last sentence in the preceding paragraph). In practice you will discover that the first sentence of the new paragraph usually does form a link with the last sentence of the old as well as with the

paragraph as a whole and does make explicit reference to the last sentence. But this is not always so. I can think of situations in which a sentence would link not with the sentence immediately preceding, but with some earlier sentence. But such situations are rare.

And too, in *conversation* our references are sometimes implicit rather than explicit. For instance, someone says: "I'm going to leave a balance in my checking account. Taxes are due next month." Here the explicit connective *because* (or *for* or *since*), showing that sentence 2 is a *reason* for sentence 1, is omitted. But you should be very cautious about allowing such omissions in your own *writing,* because they force an unaccustomed burden on the reader and often hinder his understanding.

So much for the exceptions. My father used to say that the trouble with many beginning bowlers is that they want right away to learn to bowl a curve. Don't you be like that as a beginning writer; leave the curves—the exceptions—alone for a while, and concentrate on getting a straight ball down to the pins. Study Step 6 where it lies before you in your reading and resolve to see to it that it is always incorporated into your writing.

We can turn now to further discussion of the connection of ideas and the specific reference called for in Step 6. First, the connection of ideas. Since this whole book is actually a course in the connection of ideas—in *thinking,* and thus worth your attention even if you are never called on to write—you can well imagine both that it is a big subject and that at this point we are at the very heart of the matter of thinking and writing. Let us, therefore, ask ourselves seriously how ideas can be connected.

The simplest kind of connection is *identity:* we say that one idea is actually the same as another, and we usually indicate that connection with a colon (:), which functions as an equal sign, or with an expression like *that is, that is to say that, in other words,* or *I mean.* For instance, "Prehistory is an account of something that happened before there were written records; *that is,* it is something learned about the past from unwritten ancient remains like pottery and primitive weapons." Another example: "Voting in the United States is by secret ballot; *in other words,* no one but the voter himself knows how he voted." Or, "They called my grandfather a triple-threat man; *that is,* he was outstanding as a tackler, a runner, and a passer."

The *opposite* relationship is just that: the opposite, in which we assert in the second of two sentences something contrary or con-tradictory to what we have asserted in the first. I don't mean that we contradict ourselves with something like "All triangles are equal in the sum of their angles. Not all triangles are equal in the sum of their angles." No; I mean that in the first sentence we assert something from which the reader might expect something else to be true, but which, in reality, is *not* true—as we go on to declare in the second sentence.

For instance, I say, "Most liquid substances contract, or shrink, when they freeze." Then in my next sentence I talk about the substance water, and it might be expected that I will say that it too contracts; in fact, it might be expected that I will use water as a specific example of most liquid substances. The truth is, though, that water is different: it is an exception. And so my second sentence is *"But* water expands when it freezes."

Though the word *but* (or its equivalent) may sometimes be omitted, you ought never to omit it until you become a highly experienced writer. Equivalents of *but,* which you may use instead, are *yet, still, however,* and *nevertheless.* A special equivalent of *but* is *though,* or *although,* put at the beginning of the *first* statement; if *though* is used, the two statements are put together to form one sentence. You'll find an example at the beginning of my paragraph here; for another example, look at the following two versions of the same sentence: "This book has its difficulties. *But* you can understand it if you study it carefully." "*Though* this book has its difficulties, you can understand it if you study it carefully."

We saw a special instance of this relationship in the chapter on Step 5, when we discussed the use of *true . . . but.* Another special instance will be discussed later in a chapter on comparison and *contrast.* Briefly, for now, we can say the following. In a contrast we express a difference that is not surprising or unexpected or contradictory in any way. For this reason, the connective *but* and its equivalents are not quite right (even though *and* and its equivalents would be clearly wrong). Thus it would not be quite right to say, "The American colors are red, white, and blue, but the Italian colors are red, white, and green." *But* or *however* or *nevertheless* or *although* at the beginning would suggest that we had somehow expected the two countries' colors to be the same. No, the proper connectives between contrasted assertions are *whereas* and *in contrast.* (*While* and *where* are not as good for this purpose.) Do not use *on the one hand . . . on the other hand* for this purpose, because that expression too implies a certain contradictoriness, since it means that something is being looked at from two points of view: "*On the one hand* he is presentable in appearance, *but on the other hand* not so well dressed as to intimidate simple people."

And do not try to use for this purpose, as many students do, *on the contrary. On the contrary* introduces a statement that flatly contradicts another statement or emphatically says no to a question that has been set up. For example: "Was he sober? *On the contrary,* he was so drunk he couldn't walk."

Another important relationship is expressed by the word *and* and its several equivalents: *too, also, besides, in addition, moreover, similarly, in the same way, again, furthermore, another, a similar, the same.* Now you may say, "Of course, it's a simple matter: *Jack and Jill; eat and drink.* What's the problem?"

The problem is this: in reading, when I meet a sentence in a paragraph, I want to know whether that sentence is a *new development* of the preceding idea or, instead, simply *another* example, cause, effect, detail, or whatever was in the preceding sentence. For if I don't know, I'm confused. Let me give an example.

> The concept of the circle, some people believe, is the most important of all human inventions apart from language itself. That it is an invention is clear from the fact that it is found nowhere in nature. In the form of the wheel the circle is the basis of nearly all machinery. These things, by freeing men from exclusive attention to their moment-to-moment material needs, have produced human leisure, which is the basis of culture. The circle has enabled man to discover a large portion of geometry, which in turn plays a considerable part in the development of the human mind. The poet Dante found in it a major poetic symbol. We all find in it a fascinating product of the human mind. Thus its importance as an invention, if no greater than the importance of the invention of the written word, is even more fundamental.

Before discussing this paragraph as an example of the need for the use of the word *and,* I want to clear up one or two things about the paragraph that, if they aren't cleared up, may keep distracting us from our main purpose. First, note that in his second sentence the writer has interrupted his paragraph to justify a word *(invention)* that he has used in his first sentence. That interruption, since it serves a useful purpose, is quite all right; but he might have put the interruption in parentheses (it is, after all, a parenthetical remark). And second, note that had he done so, he would have been able to use, before the third sentence, the useful connective *for.* (Had he used *for* without enclosing the second sentence in parentheses, the third sentence would seem to be a reason for the second sentence instead of the first.)

Third, the first reason the writer gives for calling the circle "important"—its function as the wheel—ought to have come *last,* for it is a far better reason than those supplied by geometry, the poetry of Dante, or even the sheer brilliance of the human mind. These, that is, come in like weak afterthoughts when they are put after, instead of before, the strongest reason.

Fourth, I think *basic* ought to have been the key word rather than *important,* since it seems to be the key notion: "The concept of the circle . . . is the most *basic* of all human inventions. . . . geometry . . . plays a *basic* part in the development of the human mind. . . . Dante found in it a *basic* poetic symbol." Of course, the writer has already called the wheel and leisure basic ("basis") and he concludes on the note of basic ("fundamental").

Now with those considerations out of the way, we can look at precisely what I have in mind: the writer says that, in the form of the wheel, the circle has led to leisure, the basis of culture. Then he says at once, "The circle has enabled man to discover a large portion of geometry, which in turn plays a considerable part in the development of the human mind."

On a first reading of this, I am at least momentarily confused. Has geometry something to do with culture, which has just been mentioned? If so, what? Or is some connection between geometry and the mechanics of the wheel being suggested? I simply do not know; and my confusion is increased when, in the next sentence, I meet Dante. For am I to connect Dante with geometry? And perhaps with the wheel as well?

Then I discover that the writer has simply done what many students do: he has thought the idea of *and* so simple that he has just omitted it! So, besides putting a *for instance* into the statement about the circle, in the form of a wheel, being basic to most machinery, I would certainly have put a *besides*, a *moreover*, or an *also* into the sentence about geometry and into the sentence about Dante—or at least begin both with an *and*. For they serve as *additional* examples, and without something like *and* or *also* the reader doesn't know that. Without *and* or *also* he is not told *what* they serve as and is left in the dark as to why, after reading about machinery, he is now reading about geometry and Dante.

No, the connections you see in your mind are so clear that you feel certain that the reader must see them clearly, too. But he doesn't see them until you get them out of your mind and down on paper. For suppose I said: "The child eats dirt and plaster. He has a condition known as pica." Now, do you know for sure whether I've said (a) that he has two ailments, a craving for nonfoods as food *and* a condition known as pica, or (b) that he eats dirt and plaster, with the result that he has become afflicted with pica, or (c) that because he has pica he has this craving for dirt and plaster?

The third choice (c) happens to be what I *meant;* but I didn't succeed in *saying* it because I omitted the connective *for* or *because.* And the need for the simple-seeming *and* (or *also,* or some other equivalent of *and*) is in many situations, as in the paragraph about the circle, as strict as the need for a *for* or a *because* in my statement about the child's pica.

As is probably already plain, when I have two successive sentences, and when sentence 1 is the result or effect and sentence 2 the cause or reason, I should connect them with *because, since, for,* or *as* (though I'd avoid this use of *as*). If the reverse is true—that is if sentence 1 is the cause or reason and sentence 2 the result or effect—I should use the connectives *therefore, so, as a result, as a consequence, thus we see,* or *it follows that.*

(Instructors who use this book and have glanced ahead to this part might someday, before the class has come to Step 6, ask their students to tell what *therefore* means. The number of students who do not know will be one index to the need for this section, in which I seem to be laboring, at length, the obvious. It is also an index to our error in teaching advanced vocabulary words before determining whether students know, for instance, the various meanings of *thus* and *but*—the little words we think with.)

I have discussed such clear-cut connectives as *and, but, therefore,* and *for.* I would like now to say a special word about the less definable connectives *in fact, indeed,* and *now.* Occasionally *in fact* is used with its basic meaning, "the fact of the matter is," or "the truth is." Thus "I thought he had given up drinking, whereas *in fact* he was drinking more than ever." More often it means "I can say even more" or "I can put the matter even more strongly or definitely." Thus: "Hla Myint's book is realistic. *In fact,* it is one of the most practical works that have appeared on southeast Asia's economy." Or: "You will not find lobelia hard to grow. *In fact,* I'll give you some seeds right now that you can take home and plant this evening." Or: "Some days the barometer will be up, but it will rain; other days it will be down, but the weather will be fair. *In fact,* you never know just by looking at the barometer whether it will rain or not." Sometimes *in fact* is used to sum things up; then it means "in short," "in brief," or "to skip over whatever else might be said."

Indeed has the same meaning as *in fact.* But *indeed* is generally reserved for more formal use; in fact, you almost never hear it in conversation except in its meaning of "certainly," as in *yes indeed* or *indeed it is* or *no indeed.*

Now, as well as meaning "at this time," is used as a connective whose meaning is a little hard to define. People say: "*Now* what is her name? I can't remember!" Or, "*Now* where did I put my glasses?" Or, "*Now* don't try to tell me that!" But *now* doesn't always lend a tone of vexation to a sentence, as in those examples; it may simply work like an exclamation point, as when Robert Browning, in "My Last

Duchess," has the Duke say "I call that piece a wonder, *now*." *Now* is indeed, though perfectly understandable, just as hard to define as the *well* in "*Well*, goodbye, Mr. Supček" and "*Well*, I can't decide whether to marry him or not."

Yet besides being one of the distinguishing features of good idiomatic spoken English, *now* is also a connective useful to a writer. First, in a syllogism I would suggest *now* as an equivalent to the Latin *atqui*, generally translated *but*. Thus we would say: "All men are mortal. *Now* Socrates is a man. Socrates, therefore, is mortal."

Second, *now* is useful when you want to say, "You have the general picture; now I want you to turn your attention to the particulars." Thus a writer of a mathematics text, having indicated that there are certain general algebraic tools, might say, "*Now* the three main kinds of variation—direct, inverse, and combined—give us a 'tool' of this kind."

Or we can use *now* for the reverse purpose of introducing a general statement arrived at by the examination of a series of particulars: "*Now* the one thing we notice about all these tests is that they test not so much the student's knowledge and understanding of the subject matter as his ability to escape the pitfalls of a tricky test."

Now is also used when for some reason a writer does not want to choose a more specific connective or wants to indicate a lack of connection. In those cases, by *now* he means something like this: "We have finished with that aspect of the subject and are turning to a new one." Thus he keeps the reader from groping for a connection between two paragraphs that simply is not there. He is saying, in effect, that he is observing Step 2 here, but that it would be inconvenient in this particular case to try to observe Step 5.

And finally, *now* can simply mean "Here is the point I wish to make" or "This is what I want to emphasize" or "I want you to give your particular attention to this."

The reason I have given such a lengthy discussion to three little words might be explained like this: whenever I've suggested that students compare their themes with printed essays and articles they read, they spontaneously and unaffectedly laugh! They think their work and professionals' work are so far apart that there is no use drawing comparisons. But I think they're wrong. That is to say, I think some of the differences between their work and professionals' work can be pinpointed, and that some of the things professionals do are quite within the ability of students. Some of the devices professionals use can be taken over by students with very little trouble—like Step 5, which after a few trials students find very easy (if they can only remember to do it). Other professional techniques, though still possible for everyone, require more work. One device that admittedly requires more work—more attention, more thinking, more time—but that can still be done by students is *the constant use of connectives*— all connectives, of course, but mainly *in fact, indeed,* and *now,* which are familiar to us in printed work but are almost never used in student work.

Now how are we to reduce all we have said about connectives to one brief rule? I think this will do: *decide what the relationship is between a sentence and the sentence preceding it; then if possible add a connective that indicates that relationship.*

For example:

> [1]Chopin knew nothing about the orchestra.
> [2]His concertos (compositions for piano and orchestra) were failures.
> [3]It is better to omit the orchestra or to fill in the orchestra part with a second piano.

Now what is the relationship between sentence 2 and sentence 1? Stop and go back and figure it out for yourself. What is it? No, don't go on to my explanation until you've figured it out. Go back.

Well, sentence 2 gives us a *result* of sentence 1, doesn't it? What are the connectives that signal a result? There are several: *therefore, so, consequently, as a consequence, as a result, it follows that.* So put one of those words in sentence 2 (someplace where it doesn't make the sentence read awkwardly).

Next, what about sentence 3? What is its relationship to sentence 2? Again, go back and decide for yourself before you read on. Again, sentence 3 is a result of sentence 2, isn't it? So put into sentence 3 also one of the words signaling a result (you probably won't want to use the same one you've just used in sentence 2). So what do you have now? You have three sentences in which ideas are connected in a relationship that has been *explained* to the reader by the use of proper connectives. And mind you, that is your very business as a writer: to show connections. For your ideas may be brilliant, or they may be very ordinary; but be they brilliant or ordinary, you are not even *writing* if you don't both have them all connected and show the reader what the connection is.

You should notice that in the example just given the relationships are those of cause and effect. As a result, instead of identifying the effect as an effect *(therefore)* you could have identified the cause as a cause. That is, it is the same to say "Chopin knew nothing about the orchestra. His concertos are, *therefore,* failures" as it is to say *"Because* Chopin knew nothing about the orchestra, his concertos are failures." Note that in the latter case the two statements are combined into one sentence.

In the example above we have had to ignore the fact that sentence 1, too, probably followed another sentence and therefore should also have had some connective word (we don't know which one) in it. We'll also ignore that fact in the examples that follow, in which you are to select the proper connective for each sentence 2, depending on its relationship with its sentence 1. Although I'll give you the correct answers later, decide now for yourself what connective you would put in sentence 2 in each of the following examples.

> [1]Last night I got my feet wet. [2]Today I have a cold.
> [1]Sam got an *F* in American history. [2]He doesn't care.
> [1]Judy got an *F* in American history. [2]She didn't study.
> [1]Jim got an *A* in American history. [2]He's on the Dean's List this semester.
> [1]I got a *C* in American history. [2]I got an *A* in chemistry.
> [1]Charles followed Steps 1, 2, and 3. [2]He used a number of excellent details and examples.
> [1]Washington is honored as the father of his country. [2]Lincoln is revered as a great leader.

Have you figured out the correct connectives? The first is *"So (therefore,* and so forth), I have a cold." Then, *"But* he doesn't care." Next, *"For* (or *because*) she didn't study." Next, *"So (therefore,* and so forth), he's on the Dean's List this semester." Next, *"But* I got an *A* in chemistry." Next, "He *also* used a number of excellent details and examples." And finally the last: "Lincoln, *too,* is revered as a great leader."

Do you get the idea? Then you can no doubt do the assignment that follows. Before giving it, however, I must take care of three objections. First, you will say that in the work of professional writers you surely don't find a connective in every sentence. There are two answers: (a) certainly, not in every sentence is a connective possible (there will always be some kind of explicit reference, though). For instance, in

"This collection consists of three sections. The first section is devoted to Romania," no connective is possible, but *the first section* does refer clearly to *three sections.* (b) after years of writing, some writers become so highly skilled that they can lead the reader successfully from thought to thought without many conventional connectives. If you too wish to develop that skill, use all the connectives you can so that in future you will have a sure feeling for which are needed and which are not.

Second, you will ask, "But can't a person use *too many* connectives?" Yes indeed, just as a person can have too many teeth. But as I've said before, I've never met a person with too many teeth; nor have I met a student who used too many connectives: all used far too few.

Third, there will be the objection "You said earlier that it would be monotonous to begin every sentence with its subject. Surely it would be monotonous to begin every sentence with a connective?" A good objection. But I think this is the answer: there is a theory (not made up just by English teachers) that the words *also, however,* and *therefore* ought not to come at the beginning of a sentence or a clause. Now I can think of several good reasons for putting that theory into practice, one of which I might approach like this: words like *if, because, and, whereas, for,* and *but* (which we call conjunctions) must come at the beginning of their sentence or clause. For instance, you can't say "I for love my work"; you must say *"For* I love my work." But expressions like *therefore, however, also* (they are perhaps oftenest used), *too, consequently,* and *besides* can come later in the sentence or clause (we call these words conjunctive adverbs). Thus "I, *however,* love my work" or "I love my work, *however."* So also "The two angles, *therefore,* are equal" or "The two angles are, *therefore,* equal." (But note that words like *however* should come first when they directly modify the word following: *"However* hard I try, I cannot give up smoking.") Putting words like *also, however,* and *therefore* someplace else besides the beginning, then, provides variety and keeps your use of connectives from becoming monotonous.

Assignment

Go patiently through as many as possible of the themes you have written, adding to each sentence, where it is possible, an appropriate connective. Do not, of course, simply stick in a number of *for example's, however's,* and *therefore's,* whether they make sense or not! Remember to distinguish between connectives that must come at the beginning of the sentence (conjunctions) and connectives you can put in after the beginning (conjunctive adverbs) in order to avoid monotony.

AN ANALYSIS

You will not realize all you can learn from Step 6 if we don't analyze, in terms of that step, a longer passage than ay we have seen so far. So let's look at such a passage in a whole essay and analyze it, and thus also provide a model for analyses you yourself can make of other passages. In the process you'll get a better insight not just into Step 6, but into the whole process of reading, writing, and thinking. For our passage to be analyzed I've chosen an article which, though it appeared over seventy-five years ago, is so well done that it has been reprinted in scores of books, a number of them on the market today. To make sure, however, that you have it before you, I've reprinted it, with paragraph numbers, in this chapter. We'll analyze parts of it to see how the author follows Step 6. (I'll also take the occasion to point out the way the author follows some other steps.)

I'd like you to read and reread this essay (actually, it was a lecture) by T. H. Huxley, in order to become familiar with it and to see whether you get Huxley's point, before we go on to our analysis. True, you may not

want to take the time either to reread it or to analyze it. But I'm reminded of the time when I objected to my dentist that I didn't have an opportunity to brush my teeth after lunch. "Oh, all right," he said. "After all, they're your teeth." So with you. After all, it's your education. It's you (with your dependents, of course) who are going to profit from all you can learn about writing and thinking. So you consider what it's worth to you and decide how much of your time you can afford to spend on this chapter.

Meanwhile, let me help you with the first two sentences in the essay below: in them the author says "expression" where you might say "application," and "mode" where you might say "way." He simply means that scientists, working in science, use the same method of reasoning (for there is, in fact, no other dependable method) that you use whenever you work at anything. "Phenomena" are anything you can see and reason about, from sunspots to a spot on your shoe. Here, then, is the article, slightly adapted.

THE METHOD OF SCIENTIFIC INVESTIGATION

by T. H. Huxley

1

The method of scientific investigation is nothing but the expression of the necessary mode of working of the human mind. It is simply the mode by which all phenomena are reasoned about and rendered precise and exact. There is no more difference, but there is just the same kind of difference, between the mental operations of a man of science and those of an ordinary person, as there is between the operations and methods of a baker or of a butcher weighing out his goods in common scales, and the operations of a chemist in performing a difficult and complex analysis by means of his balance and finely graduated weights. It is not that the action of the scales in the one case, and the balance in the other, differ in the principles of their construction or manner or working; but the beam of one is set on an infinitely finer axis than the other, and of course turns by the addition of a much smaller weight.

2

You will understand this better, perhaps, if I give you a familiar example. You have all heard it repeated, I dare say, that men of science work by means of induction and deduction, and that by the help of these operations, they, in a sort of sense, wring from Nature certain other things, which are called natural laws, and causes, and that out of these, by some cunning skill of their own, they build up hypotheses and theories. And it is imagined by many, that the operations of the common mind can be by no means compared with these processes, and that they have to be acquired by a sort of special apprenticeship to the craft. To hear all these large words, you would think that the mind of a man of science must be constituted differently from that of his fellow men; but if you will not be frightened by terms, you will discover that you are quite wrong, and that all these terrible apparatus are being used by yourselves every day and every hour of your lives.

3

There is a well-known incident in one of Molière's plays, where the author makes the hero express unbounded delight on being told that he had been talking prose during the whole of his life. In the same way, I trust, you will take comfort, and be delighted with yourselves, on the discovery that you have been acting on the principles of inductive and deductive philosophy during the same period. Probably there is not one here who has not in the course of the day had occasion to set in motion a complex train of reasoning, of the very same kind, though differing of course in degree, as that which a scientific man goes through in tracing the causes of natural phenomena.

4

A very trivial circumstance will serve to exemplify this. Suppose you go into a fruiterer's shop, wanting an apple—you take up one, and, on biting it, you find it is sour; you look at it, and see that it is hard and green. You take up another one, and that too is hard, green, and sour. The shopman

THE METHOD OF SCIENTIFIC INVESTIGATION From Thomas H. Huxley, "Phenomena of Organic Nature," *Darwiniana* (New York: D. Appleton and Company, 1904), pp. 363–75.

STEP 6: AN ANALYSIS

offers you a third; but, before biting it, you examine it, and find that it is hard and green, and you immediately say that you will not have it, as it must be sour, like those that you have already tried.

5

Nothing can be more simple than that, you think; but if you will take the trouble to analyze and trace out into its logical elements what has been done by the mind, you will be greatly surprised. In the first place, you have performed the operation of induction. You found that, in two experiences, hardness and greenness in apples went together with sourness. It was so in the first case, and it was confirmed by the second. True, it is a very small basis, but still it is enough to make an induction from; you generalize the facts, and you expect to find sourness in apples where you get hardness and greenness. You found upon that a general law, that all hard and green apples are sour; and that, so far as it goes, is a perfect induction. Well, having got your natural law in this way, when you are offered another apple which you find is hard and green, you say, "All hard and green apples are sour; this apple is hard and green, therefore this apple is sour." That train of reasoning is what logicians call a syllogism, and has all its various parts and terms—its major premise, its minor premise, and its conclusion. And, by the help of further reasoning, which, if drawn out, would have to be exhibited in two or three other syllogisms, you arrive at your final determination, "I will not have that apple." So that, you see, you have, in the first place, established a law by induction, and upon that you have founded a deduction, and reasoned out the special conclusion of the particular case. Well now, suppose, having got your law, that at some time afterwards, you are discussing the qualities of apples with a friend: you will say to him, "It is a very curious thing, but I find that all hard and green apples are sour!" Your friend says to you, "But how do you know that?" You at once reply, "Oh, because I have tried them over and over again, and have always found them to be so." Well, if we were talking science instead of common sense, we should call that an experimental verification. And, if still opposed, you go further, and say, "I have heard from the people in Somersetshire and Devonshire, where a large number of apples are grown, that they have observed the same thing. It is also found to be the case in Normandy, and in North America. In short, I find it to be the universal experience of mankind wherever attention has been directed to the subject." Whereupon, your friend, unless he is a very unreasonable man, agrees with you, and is convinced that you are quite right in the conclusion you have drawn. He believes, although perhaps he does not know he believes it, that the more extensive verifications are—that the more frequently experiments have been made, and results of the same kind arrived at—that the more varied the conditions under which the same results are attained, the more certain is the ultimate conclusion, and he disputes the question no further. He sees that the experiment has been tried under all sorts of conditions, as to time, place, and people, with the same result; and he says with you, therefore, that the law you have laid down must be a good one and he must believe it.

6

In science we do the same thing; the scientist exercises precisely the same faculties, though in a much more delicate manner. In scientific inquiry it becomes a matter of duty to expose a supposed law to every possible kind of verification, and to take care, moreover, that this is done intentionally, and not left to a mere accident, as in the case of the apples. And in science, as in common life, our confidence in a law is in exact proportion to the absence of variation in the result of our experimental verifications. For instance, if you let go your grasp of some object you may have in your hand, it will immediately fall to the ground. That is a very common verification of one of the best established laws of nature—that of gravitation. The method by which men of science establish the existence of that law is exactly the same as that by which we have established the trivial proposition about the sourness of hard and green apples. But we believe it in such an extensive, thorough, and unhesitating manner because the universal experience of mankind verifies it, and we can verify it ourselves at any time; and that is the strongest possible foundation on which any natural law can rest.

7

So much, then, by way of proof that the method of establishing laws in science is exactly the same as that pursued in common life. Let us now turn to another matter (though really it is but another phase of the same question), and that is, the method by which, from the relations of certain phenomena, we prove that some stand in the position of causes towards the others.

8

I want to put the case clearly before you, and I will therefore show you what I mean by another familiar example. I will suppose that one of you, on coming down in the morning to the parlor of your house, finds that a silver teapot and some spoons which had been left in the room on the previous evening are gone—the window is open, and you observe the mark of a dirty hand on the window frame, and perhaps, in addition to that, you notice the impress of a hobnailed shoe on the gravel outside. All these phenomena have struck your attention instantly, and before two seconds have passed you say, "Oh, somebody has broken open the window, entered the room, and run off with the spoons and the teapot!" That speech is out of your mouth in a moment. And you will probably add, "I know he has; I am quite sure of it!" You mean to say exactly what you know; but in reality you are giving expression to what is, in all essential particulars, a hypothesis. You do not *know* it at all; it is nothing but a hypothesis rapidly framed in your own mind. And it is a hypothesis founded on a long train of inductions and deductions.

9

What are those inductions and deductions, and how have you got at this hypothesis? You have observed, in the first place, that the window is open; but by a train of reasoning involving many inductions and deductions, you have probably arrived long before at the general law—and a very good one it is—that windows do not open of themselves; and you therefore conclude that something has opened the window. A second general law that you have arrived at in the same way is, that teapots and spoons do not go out of a window spontaneously, and you are satisfied that, as they are not now where you left them, they have been removed. In the third place, you look at the marks on the window sill, and the shoemarks outside, and you say that in all previous experience the former kind of mark has never been produced by anything else but the hand of a human being; and the same experience shows that no other animal but man at present wears shoes with hobnails in them such as would produce the marks in the gravel. I do not know, even if we could discover any of those "missing links" that are talked about, that they would help us to any other conclusion! At any rate the law which states our present experience is strong enough for my present purpose. You next reach the conclusion that, as these kinds of marks have not been left by any other animal than man, nor are liable to be formed in any other way than by a man's hand and shoe, the marks in question have been formed by a man in that way. You have, further, a general law, founded on observation and experience, and that, too, is, I am sorry to say, a very universal and unimpeachable one—that some men are thieves; and you assume at once from all these premises—and that is what constitutes your hypothesis—that the man who made the marks outside and on the window sill, opened the window, got into the room, and stole your teapot and spoons. You have now arrived at a *vera causa* (a reasonable judgment); you have assumed a cause which, it is plain, is competent to produce all the phenomena you have observed. You can explain all these phenomena only by the hypothesis of a thief. But that is a hypothetical conclusion, of the justice of which you have no absolute proof at all; it is only rendered highly probable by a series of inductive and deductive reasonings.

10

I suppose your first action, assuming that you are a man of ordinary common sense, and that you have established this hypothesis to your own satisfaction, will very likely be to go off for the police, and set them on the track of the burglar, with the view to the recovery of your property. But just as you are starting with this object, some person comes in, and on learning what you are about, says, "My good friend, you are going on a great deal too fast. How do you know that the man who really made the marks took the spoons? It might have been a monkey that took them, and the man may have merely looked in afterwards." You would probably reply, "Well, that is all very well, but you see it is contrary to all experience of the way teapots and spoons are abstracted; so that, at any rate, your hypothesis is less probable than mine." While you are talking the thing over in this way, another friend arrives, one of that good kind of people that I was talking of a little while ago. And he might say, "Oh, my dear sir, you are certainly going on a great deal too fast. You are most presumptuous. You admit that all these occurrences took place when you were fast asleep, at a time when you could not possibly have known anything about what was taking place. How do you know that the laws of Nature are not suspended during the night? It may be that there has been some kind of supernatural interference in this case." In point of fact, he declares that your hypothesis is one of which you cannot at all demonstrate the truth, and that you are by no means sure that the laws of Nature are the same when you are asleep as when you are awake.

11

Well, now, you cannot at the moment answer that kind of reasoning. You feel that your worthy friend has you somewhat at a disadvantage. You will feel perfectly convinced in your own mind, however, that you are quite right, and you say to him, "My good friend, I can only be guided by the natural probabilities of the case, and if you will be kind enough to stand aside and permit me to pass, I will go and fetch the police." Well, we will suppose that your journey is successful, and that by good luck you meet with a policeman; that eventually the burglar is found with your property on his person, and the marks correspond to his hand and to his boots. Probably any jury would consider those facts a very good experimental verification of your hypothesis, touching the cause of the abnormal phenomena observed in your parlor, and would act accordingly.

12

Now, in this suppositious case, I have taken phenomena of a very common kind, in order that you might see what are the different steps in an ordinary process of reasoning, if you will only take the trouble to analyze it carefully. All the operations I have described, you will see, are involved in the mind of any man of sense in leading him to a conclusion as to the course he should take in order to make good a robbery and punish the offender. I say that you are led, in that case, to your conclusion by exactly the same train of reasoning as that which a man of science pursues when he is endeavoring to discover the origin and laws of the most occult phenomena. The process is, and always must be, the same; and precisely the same mode of reasoning was employed by Newton and Laplace in their endeavors to discover and define the causes of the movements of the heavenly bodies, as you, with your own common sense, would employ to detect a burglar. The only difference is that, the nature of the inquiry being more abstruse, every step has to be most carefully watched, so that there may not be a single crack or flaw in your hypothesis. A flaw or crack in many of the hypotheses of daily life may be of little or no moment as affecting the general correctness of the conclusions at which we may arrive; but, in a scientific inquiry, a fallacy, great or small, is always of importance, and is sure to be in the long run constantly productive of mischievous, if not fatal results.

13

Do not allow yourselves to be misled by the common notion that a hypothesis is untrustworthy simply because it is a hypothesis. It is often urged, in respect to some scientific conclusion, that, after all, it is only a hypothesis. But what more have we to guide us in nine-tenths of the most important affairs of daily life than hypotheses, and often very ill-based ones? So that in science, where the evidence of a hypothesis is subjected to the most rigid examination, we may rightly pursue the same course. You may have hypotheses, and hypotheses. A man may say, if he likes, that the moon is made of green cheese: that is a hypothesis. But another man, who has devoted a great deal of time and attention to the subject, and availed himself of the most powerful telescopes and the results of the observations of others, declares that in his opinion it is probably composed of materials very similar to those of which our own earth is made up: and that is also only a hypothesis. But I need not tell you that there is an enormous difference in the value of the two hypotheses. That one which is based on sound scientific knowledge is sure to have a corresponding value; and that which is a mere hasty random guess is likely to have but little value. Every great step in our progress in discovering causes has been made in exactly the same way as that which I have detailed to you. A person observing the occurrence of certain facts and phenomena asks, naturally enough, what process, what kind of operation known to occur in Nature applied to the particular

STEP 6: AN ANALYSIS

case, will unravel and explain the mystery? Hence you have the scientific hypothesis; and its value will be proportionate to the care and completeness with which its basis has been tested and verified. It is in these matters as in the commonest affairs of practical life; the guess of the fool will be folly, while the guess of the wise man will contain wisdom. In all cases, you see that the value of the result depends on the patience and faithfulness with which the investigator applies to his hypothesis every possible kind of verification.

ANALYSIS

First, of course, let's see how, in paragraph 1, the second sentence is related to the first according to Step 6. I'm sorry that you'll have to keep turning back to the essay (as you'd have to keep turning back to the microscope if you were drawing a picture of a paramecium in biology lab), but you'll find doing so worth the effort. So let's proceed: "it," a pronoun, in sentence 2 means "the method of scientific investigation" in sentence 1. "Is" in sentence 2 simply is synonymous with "is nothing but" in sentence 1. "The mode by which *all* phenomena" in sentence 2 repeats the word "mode" in sentence 1, and "by which *all* phenomena" in sentence 2 means the same as "necessary" in sentence 1—just as, for instance, since *all* routes to San Marino pass through Italy, travel through (or over) Italy is the *necessary* mode of reaching San Marino. "Reasoned about and rendered precise and exact" is synonymous with "working of the human mind."

But we have just shown, haven't we, that the second sentence means the same as the first—matches it term for term? In a moment we'll show that the third sentence does the same thing. Meanwhile, it would be useful for you to reread the essay to see how, as Huxley goes on, in sentence after sentence, in paragraph after paragraph, he keeps repeating the same idea, changing only the details and the comparisons. Just for example (and it is not the first you can find), when he says in paragraph 2 that all those terrible apparatus (used in the scientific method) are used by you every hour of your lives, what he is saying boils down to the fact that scientists think like you—scientific thinking is only ordinary human thinking—which is what the first sentence of the essay boils down to.

But I want you yourself to go through every sentence up to paragraph 7, to see how many times Huxley, in one way or another, whatever details he adds or comparisons he uses, is simply making again and again the point that scientists think like everybody else—that the method of scientific investigation is nothing but the method of thinking that you have been using all day, every day, since infancy. *Did you notice on your first reading or readings how he keeps repeating that point?* The point that scientists think like you do is, in effect, Huxley's sentence X (his first sentence); and this will become totally obvious to you as you go through the first seven paragraphs.

In fact, it is important to a successful reading of this famous essay for you to grasp that that *is* Huxley's point, because most students (and, I fear, some instructors) read it exactly backwards. They think Huxley is saying, "You too can think like a scientist." Precisely not; Huxley says that since you already do think, and have always thought, like a scientist, scientists think like you and must do so, for there is no other dependable way of thinking.

Why he chooses to make this point to his audience is something we'll come to later. Meanwhile, simply realize that he does *not* begin his essay with a sentence X like "The ordinary man in the street can learn, and can apply in his daily life, the method of scientific investigation used by scientists in reaching their hypotheses and forming their conclusions." No! To repeat, his very point is that since the ordinary man in the street (when he is acting rationally, as the essay later implies) *already* uses, has always used, and can do nothing else but use the method of scientific investigation, then scientists studying fossils are doing exactly what you are doing when you are figuring out how a spot got on your shoe.

Now that you've reread the article to paragraph 7, as I asked you to, let's continue our analysis where we left off. In sentence 3, "there is no more difference" is the same as "is simply" in sentence 2 (and, of course, as "nothing but" in sentence 1). In sentence 3, "mental operations of a man of science" is equivalent to "it" in sentence 2, which, as we saw, means "the method of scientific investigation" in sentence 1. "Those of the ordinary person" in sentence 3 is equivalent to "all phenomena are reasoned about" (that is, "including those that the ordinary person reasons about") in sentence 2.

"Yes," you say. "Now what about 'but there is just the same kind of *difference*' in sentence 3? Huxley seems to be saying that the two *are* different." No. The explanation, I'm afraid, will be a little long. First, do not forget that from the very first sentence Huxley has asserted that the two are the same. Second, he begins his third sentence with "there is no more difference," which implies that any difference is outweighed by the similarity. Third, he is telling us that the similarity is *essential* and the difference only *accidental.* What does that mean?

Huxley explains it in the next sentence in terms of two weighing devices, when he says that they do not differ in construction or in manner of working (*that* is the essential), but only in fineness of measurement (which is accidental). Similarly, if I show you a tray of gems and tell you they're all diamonds, you don't disagree with me because some of the stones are *larger* than some of the others. *That* difference is just accidental. To put it in another way, a scientist's thinking and your thinking are the same qualitatively—that is, in kind; they differ only quantitatively—that is, in degree (here, in degree of carefulness).

But fourth, you must understand why Huxley confuses the issue by introducing this accidental difference. Thereby hangs a tale. A moment ago I said that later we'd look into the reason *why* Huxley chose to make the point that scientists think like us. The reason is that he wanted to defend Darwin's hypothesis of evolution through natural selection; and this motive affected his lecture in several ways. First of all, of course, his argument is that scientists do not arrive at their conclusions (read "Darwin did not arrive at his hypothesis") by some kind of mumbo-jumbo or by some process too highly complicated for the ordinary person to judge, but by the same mental processes ordinary people use in their daily lives. "Since you *trust* yourself," Huxley says in effect, "when you reason about, say, the disappearance of a teapot, then you should trust scientists (read 'Darwin') when, using the same processes you do, they reach conclusions in their field (read 'the origin of species through natural selection')."

Second, Huxley takes pains to defend hypotheses; for that is what Darwin's conclusion was—a hypothesis. "You trust your hypotheses in your daily life," he says in effect. "Why not, then, trust scientists' hypotheses (Darwin's hypothesis)?"

Third, if we answer that some of our reasonable hypotheses prove, in the end, false, Huxley tells us that scientists reason far more carefully about science than we (or they, for the matter) do about the ordinary problems of daily life. And *that* is why he introduces, even in his first paragraph, the for-some-readers confusing quantitative difference noted above. He is saying, in effect, "You can put a double faith in scientists: first, they use your own trustworthy methods of thinking, and second, they use them even more carefully than you do."

By the way, that Huxley is somewhat defensive about hypotheses is the reason he ends by saying that the guess of a fool will be folly while the guess of a wise man will contain wisdom and that the value of a hypothesis depends on verification—which, because he puts it last, some readers have taken to be his sentence X. But I do not intend to argue here either against or for the hypothesis of natural selection.

And Huxley's lecture will be just as illustrative if you apply it to the Bohr theory or to Planck's quantum theory instead of to Darwinism; in fact, Huxley himself applies it to Newton and Laplace.

Thus, to sum up, you see why Huxley, emphasizing that two things are the same, introduces at the same time a difference—and thus, I fear, confuses some readers.

Now before asking you to do, on your own, some of this analysis of Huxley's essay in accordance with Step 6, I want to take up a few particular matters with you myself. The first thing I want to take up with you is the interesting paragraph 2. Look at the sentence "You have all heard it repeated, I dare say, that men of science work by means of induction and deduction, and that . . . *by some cunning skill of their own,* they build up hypotheses and theories." Now, most of that sentence is equivalent to "the method of scientific investigation" in the first sentence of the essay, for the method of scientific investigation is exactly what Huxley is describing. We should therefore expect the remainder of the sentence—"by some cunning skill of their own"—to match the latter part of the first sentence of the essay: "nothing but the expression of the necessary mode of working of the human mind." But "by some cunning skill of their own" means the very opposite! It means that scientists operate not like ordinary men, but by some different, specially acquired mode of reasoning.

Is Huxley contradicting himself? Or is the hasty reader right when he says Huxley's essay means "You too can think like a scientist if you work hard at it"? Look at the expression "you have all heard it repeated, I dare say." Then look at "and it is imagined by many," in the next sentence—which goes on to say, in reverse order, the very clear opposite of the first sentence of the essay by saying that "the operations of the common mind can be *by no means* compared with these processes," and that "they *have to be acquired* by a sort of *special apprenticeship* to the craft." Look as carefully at "to hear all these large words, you would think" in the next sentence, and note that it is followed by an even firmer contradiction—an outright denial—of what Huxley said in the first sentence of his essay: "The mind of a man of science must be constituted differently from that of his fellow men."

What *is* Huxley doing here? Contradicting himself? No. The expressions "you have all heard it repeated, I dare say," "it is imagined by many," and "to hear all these large words, you would think" are *connectives*—connectives that indicate that Huxley is presenting actual or possible *objections* to *his* assertion that scientists think just like the rest of us. And then remember, above all, that connectives like this—connectives that present the opposing side of the argument—introduce statements that must eventually be followed by a statement that begins with *but* (or some equivalent). Is that the case in Huxley's paragraph 2? Look back at the essay and see.

Yes, and after "but" Huxley not only returns to an assertion of his own argument—"all these terrible apparatus are being used by *yourselves*"—but handles the refutation of the opposing argument (Huxley's method of refutation is to prove *his* point by giving the examples that follow).

Note as well that Huxley does not introduce the objections with a connective like *true* or *I grant*. He might have used such connectives in his *first* paragraph—"true, scientists are more painstaking" or "I grant, there is a difference of degree." But here the objections, or arguments contrary to his own, are *not* true (in fact he says "you are quite wrong"). So Huxley uses equivalents of *some people say,* which lead us at least to suspect that eventually he is going to say, "but they are wrong, because. . . ."

Perhaps you think that this analysis is tedious. But I honestly believe that many people cannot read successfully because they have never been taught to understand and pay attention to *connectives,* not the least important of which is the *true . . . but, some people say . . . but* variety, which appears very often in sophisticated writing.

Finally, let me point out that Huxley makes his article more interesting by introducing a *conflict,* which he sets up by bringing in imaginary objections. In doing so, he must use the *connectives* that are proper to objections. We'll apply both conflict and connectives to your own writing later, in the chapter on the argumentative paper. Meanwhile, we must get on with our analysis.

The second thing I want to take up with you is paragraph 7. It's extremely interesting. First, notice that though it appears in type as a paragraph, it is hardly a paragraph properly speaking, for it has only two sentences and little development. This kind of paragraph is often called a transitional paragraph. Its only function (*transition* means "a going across") is to lead the reader from one section of an essay to the next section *without confusion:* it explains to him, in effect, *both* that he should be ready for a change in thought (so he won't say: "Weren't we talking about such and such? What are we doing now?") *and* that the new thought is connected with the old.

Moreover, Huxley's transitional paragraph does what transitional paragraphs often do: it begins by *summarizing* what has been said so far: "the method of establishing laws in science is exactly the same as that pursued in common life." And in this case we see that what has been said so far is, of course, what has been said in sentence X. (By the way, the word *exactly* ought to remove from your mind any doubts raised by the merely quantitative difference spoken of in paragraph 1. In other words, scientists do think just like you.)

I said this transitional paragraph is extremely interesting. For it is a little lesson in composition all by itself (except that, naturally, it lacks detail). It is so first because it takes the time and trouble to tell the reader where he has been, where he is now, and where he is going; second, because it succinctly puts the *point* into words and lets the reader know that it *is* the point; and third, because its very purpose is to show the connection of ideas—*which is what writing is all about.*

True, the papers you are writing now are too short to need transitional paragraphs—they would be as much out of proportion in your theme as a paragraph of introduction or of conclusion would be. But not only will you someday be writing long papers, in which you may be using paragraphs of transition; you are, right now, making brief transitional devices out of every topic sentence except the first. For your topic sentences now make a reference to the old paragraph, besides introducing the new; show how the two paragraphs are connected; and thus indicate to the reader the direction he is to be following (all part of Step 5).

In fact—and this is Step 6—in a way *every* sentence is a little transitional sentence, for as we've seen, besides introducing its own new material, *every* sentence must make an explicit reference to the preceding sentence and indicate how it is connected to the preceding sentence, thus alerting the reader to the path he will be following.

Combining all that we have said now about transitions, we can formulate the following rules.. First, in long themes introduce each new section with a paragraph that summarizes both the old and the new sections and indicates the connection between the two. Second, in every section and in every theme introduce each paragraph with a sentence that refers to the preceding paragraph, introduces the idea of the new paragraph, and indicates the connection between the two. Third, in every paragraph make each sentence refer to the preceding sentence, present its own material, and indicate the connection between the two. Thus the whole theme is thoroughly connected. That —and nothing but that—is *writing,* in the true sense of the word.

If we return now to Step 6 specifically, it may be interesting to analyze Huxley's paragraph 3, where he actually invites us to match sentence with sentence. In sentence 2 he does so first of all with the logical connective "in the same way." Then "you," in sentence 2, matches "hero" in sentence 1. Next, "take comfort, and be delighted with yourselves" in sentence 2 matches "express unbounded delight" in sentence 1. "On the discovery that" in sentence 2 matches "on being told that" in sentence 1. "You have been acting on the principles of inductive and deductive philosophy" in sentence 2 matches "had been talking prose" in sentence 1, and "during the same period" in sentence 2 matches "during the whole of his life" in sentence 1.

Assignment

I will leave you to analyze the connection of the third sentence of paragraph 3 with the second sentence. That's a little harder! But the main part of your assignment is this: analyze paragraphs 5 and 12 of Huxley's essay in regard to Step 6. Find every connection you can; by no means be satisfied with one if you can find more. In paragraph 5, do not miss the connection between "your friend" and "you" and between "says" and "reply"; they are, broadly speaking, antonyms (that is, they *contrast,* and contrast is an important form of connection). And do not miss the *true . . . but* construction in that paragraph. In Paragraph 12, do not miss the fact that Huxley is *still* saying what he was saying in paragraph 1. In both, do not miss the opportunity of seeing how Step 5 is also involved.

And Step 4? Do you find that in these paragraphs, as in the others, Huxley is being specific and concrete in the explanation of his general and abstract assertions? Does he go into detail? Does he give examples? Does he not actually say a lot about *one thing?*

Your instructor will give you more than one day for this assignment. It is a long one. At the same time, you may wish to analyze more of the essay than has been assigned. That's good, because this may be the most important assignment of your writing (and reading) career.

Above all, I want you to learn from this assignment that writing is *not* just putting down one sentence after another, as bricks are laid. It is more like knitting than bricklaying, in that each new sentence—like each new row of stitches—is created by hooking the new thread *into* the old. *That* is the way *writing* is done (anything else is mere amateur scribbling). And that is the way *reading* is done: we see where each new sentence has got us precisely by seeing exactly how it has departed from the old; we see the real point the writer is making with each new sentence only when we see the connection between it and the sentence before it. All this may be painfully slow for you at first; when it becomes a habit, you will hardly have to think about it.

CONTRAST

When students try to write a theme (or perhaps just a paragraph) in which they have to *contrast* two people, two things, two poems, and so forth, they usually make certain mistakes. And their mistakes are so basic that the compositions they write are simply unacceptable. I have found by long experience, however, that if they learn a few rules designed to prevent those basic mistakes, then without much difficulty they can write acceptable contrasts. So if the rules that follow in this chapter seem odd to you, just remember that they serve the practical purpose of preventing the serious mistakes that, without them, students nearly always make.

But you are probably half wondering why, out of all the possible kinds of composition, we are making a special bother about contrast. I must, therefore, answer that question before going on to the rules. And the first explanation is this: contrast is one of the two kinds of composition with which students have special trouble (the other is argumentation). We must, therefore, remove that trouble.

The second reason for studying contrast is that the very process of

contrast has special values; and writing themes involving it is therefore especially useful practice. For one thing, when you seem to be
unable to think of much to say about a man, a situation, a poem, or a
short musical composition, you can try contrasting it with another in
the same category. Then suddenly there may be a lot to say. For
instance, what can I say about Uncle Ed? Not much, it seems—until I
conceive the idea of contrasting him with Uncle Joe, and then many
things spring to my mind. This is because the process of contrast gives
a special focus to our vision of something, so that by using it we realize
possibilities of analysis that would otherwise not occur to us.

So true is this, in fact, that we can sometimes analyze something
more successfully if we contrast it with a purely imagined difference.
We can, for example, better understand how the first words of
Lincoln's Gettysburg Address set the tone of the speech if we *imagine*
that Lincoln had begun, instead, with the words *eighty-seven years
ago.*

There is a reason the process of contrast is so stimulating and productive. It is that fundamentally we perceive through differences (and through similarities, about which we'll say something in a few minutes). The very reason that qualities like generosity and bravery come to our attention is that they are different from stinginess and cowardice. The *tone* of any composition, like the Gettysburg Address, would never be noticed if the tone of one did not strike our attention by differing from the tone of another. (It was because *everything* in everybody's experience tended to fall earthward—even steam is relatively earthbound—that nobody paid much attention to gravitation until Isaac Newton had his curious insight into it.)

For even in the physical realm we perceive by contrast. We can read, for instance, because the black letters contrast with the white page (or the light chalk with the dark blackboard). The reason we can't see in the dark is that everything is black, with no contrast.

Since we are coming later to a similarly valuable process—comparison—let's take the opportunity here to say that we also perceive through similarities. As children, we see in the world around us a number of petaled, colored, fairly round, often fragrant things that typically appear amid greenery; we note how they are similar, and forming the concept that we call *flower,* we apply it to all flowers, both familiar and new. Later, when we are college students, we are able to understand *magneto* if someone tells us it is *like* a generator. (Actually, students would probably be told that a magneto is like a generator *but* has a permanent magnet. This addition of difference to similarity produces the valuable thing called a *definition,* which we have already talked about.) In fact, if I tell you I have a blue sweater, you understand me because you have seen blue, and sweaters, before!

But we must return to the advantages of making a special study of contrast. The third reason is the very practical one that in our school-work and elsewhere we will often be called on to contrast two American presidents, two kinds of social welfare laws, Haggada and Halakha, a percept and a concept, a sacrament and a sacramental, a symbol and a metaphor. And experience shows that in so doing we may meet trouble if we haven't mastered a few simple rules.

First, select for treatment differences that make a difference—that is, significant differences, meaningful differences. Do not be like one of my students who, when asked to contrast college and high school, wrote that in high school all the buildings had been of one story, whereas in college he found that the buildings had two stories. But notice that students who write that in college one must pay tuition or fees (whereas in high school one does not) may not be doing much better. Since actually some colleges are tuition-free, while some high schools charge tuition, the difference these student writers choose can hardly be an essential one! Or isn't it? Since *most* colleges charge tuition and most high schools do not, do you think students tend to prize more highly education for which they pay than education they get for free? If so, say so; that is, *if the difference you select is not obviously significant, explain its significance.*

Second, do not say, "Oranges are round, whereas bananas are yellow." There you are contrasting a shape with a color. To do so is meaningless. If shape is to be the basis of your comparison, it must be so for both of the things contrasted: oranges are round, whereas bananas are oblong. If color is the basis: oranges are orange, whereas bananas are yellow.

And in the same way, neither can you say that Julia is quiet, whereas Hazel is selfish. If degree of talkativeness is the basis of the contrast, *Julia is quiet* must be matched by *whereas Hazel is talkative* if there is to be a contrast. In the same way, if degree of givingness is the basis, *whereas Hazel is selfish* must be matched by *Julia is generous.*

The third rule is really the same as the second rule, but it gets at the matter in a different way. It is this: you do not have a *contrast* when you have merely said something *different* about two people or things; you must say about one the *opposite* of what you have said about the other. For instance, before I started giving students instructions in the writing of contrasts, I'd call for a paper contrasting two characters in Ibsen's play *Hedda Gabler* and get themes like this.

> Thea led a closely protected life, even after she came out into the world somewhat by marrying the sheriff. But Hedda had been her father's pride and joy and had possibly been spoiled by him.

I used to puzzle over paper after paper like that trying to find what *contrast* the writers may have had in mind, until finally I realized that my students *thought* they had a contrast because they were saying *one* thing about Thea and *another* thing about Hedda!

No! If I say that Thea's life was *protected,* then I must say the *opposite* about Hedda's life. I must, that is, say that Hedda's life was *not* protected—or some equivalent: Hedda came and went as she pleased, or Hedda's father let her mix freely in society, or Hedda's father felt she must learn the ways of the world. In other words, I must say something that adds up to the fact that Hedda was unprotected (since the other part of my contrast was that Thea was *protected*). Or, if I want to keep what I said about Hedda's being her father's pride and joy and being spoiled, I have to say the *opposite* about Thea. I must, that is, indicate that Thea was *not* her father's pride and joy and was *not* spoiled.

In fact, recall what we said about *antonyms* when we were talking about the forms of explicit reference. For are we not saying that every contrast is built on a word and some kind of antonym for that word —*hot-cold, big-little, visible-invisible, cooperative-uncooperative?*

I must direct your attention here, however, to the fact that the antonyms I've just given are antonyms strictly speaking. They are direct opposites, or what logicians call *contradictories.* What logicians call *contraries* are simply differences *in the same line*—or, as we say, differences *having the same base*. Thus *red* and *not red* are clear contradictories; they are direct opposites; they are in the category of antonyms. But *red* and *green* are a somewhat different case; we think of green as a different color from red, certainly, but we never say that it is the direct opposite of red. We can think of it as non-red, because it is simply a different color from red. And the two *do* form a *contrast,* certainly.

"Well," you may say, "aren't you admitting now what you denied a moment ago? Isn't *spoiled* (which we said of Hedda) quite *different* from *protected* (which we said of Thea)? Yes, it is. But *spoiled* and *protected* are not in the same line; they do not have the same base. We can no more make any meaningful relationship between them than we could between a frying pan and the Statue of Liberty. "Red is not green" is meaningful; but "Spoiled is not protected" or "Protected is not spoiled" is not. And here is a final test: a thing cannot be green and red in the same way at the same time; thus red and green can be contrasted. But a person *can* be both spoiled and protected (or unspoiled and unprotected, as the case may be) in the same way at the same time; *spoiled* and *protected,* therefore, can hardly be contrasted.

Fourth, when you are contrasting two persons or things, nothing that is not a contrast belongs in your material. In other words, you cannot say that Hedda is selfish and then go on to something else about Hedda, ignoring Thea. You must, instead, then say the *opposite* thing about Thea. That is, when you have said that Hedda is selfish and illustrated her selfishness by accounts of her conduct with other characters, you must then say that Thea is unselfish, or generous or altruistic and proceed to illustrate her selfishness. In other words, you can't say Hedda is selfish, illustrate her selfishness, and then go on to talk about her appearance and dress without first taking up *Thea* and her *unselfishness.*

Fifth, take up things, always, in the order in which you first present them. Don't say "Tom is different from Harry. Harry is. . . ." No, say "Tom is different from Harry. *Tom* is . . ." because you introduced Tom first. And *keep* Tom first throughout.

The sixth rule is a different kind of rule, since it has to do only with vocabulary. First, *contrast* and *comparison* (which we will come to) are names of the operations you perform; they are *not* words that you are to use in your theme as synonyms for *difference* and *likeness* (except for the expression *in contrast*). That is, do not say "There are many contrasts between Thea and Hedda" or "there is another comparison between Theodore Roosevelt and Franklin Roosevelt." Instead, use such words as *difference, dissimilarity, likeness, similarity,* and *resemblance.*

As connectives in contrasts, do *not* use the expressions *on the contrary, on the other hand,* and *where.* I am repeating here, of course, some of what I said earlier, in connection with connectives. As you may remember, I said that *on the contrary* is used not for a contrast, but for a *denial:* "The common assertion is that people thought the world was flat. On the contrary, they were thoroughly convinced that it was round." Or, "Is it difficult? On the contrary; it is quite easy." *On the other hand* is used not in contrasting two persons or things, but in introducing another point of view of the same thing or situation. "He is never on time for work; on the other hand, when he does get here he sells more than our other salesmen put together."

The proper connectives for contrasts are *whereas* and *in contrast.* Thus, "Hedda is selfish, *whereas* Thea is altruistic." Or, "The Duke values things that he can possess while others cannot. The Duchess, *in contrast,* places no value whatever on ownership." (Please notice that *whereas* has no comma after it, any more than any other subordinating conjunction, like *if* or *because; whereas* followed by a comma is an old-fashioned expression meaning "because," used only in formal proclamations.) *While* is a conversational substitute for *whereas.* Thus, "Thea is generous, *while* Hedda is selfish." But do not use *where* for *whereas,* as in "John is scrupulously honest where Andy is not above helping himself to office stationery and stamps."

All that has been said of contrast can be said, *mutatis mutandis* (which you'll find in the dictionary), about *comparison.* Comparison is of likenesses, of course, whereas contrast is of differences. (Somewhat confusingly, our language uses "compare *to*" for likeness and "compare *with*" for difference: "Shall I compare thee *to* a summer's day?" "Compared *with* wisdom, gold and silver are as a little sand.")

Thus one can compare lemons and grapefruit (both are citrus fruits), detailing their similarities; or one can compare Shelley and Keats (both Romantic poets), pianos and harpsichords (both keyboard instruments), or the government of Canada and the government of Australia.

Of course, things described as *similar* are never *identical,* else there would be no point in spending time in comparing them. Nobody ever said more of the proverbial two peas in a pod than that they are virtually wholly alike! In other words, things people spend time in comparing are, while alike, also unlike. (It may interest you to know that finding similarities amid differences is the quality of genius, according to Aristotle—himself a genius.) One of the delights of poetry rests on this quality of comparison. The reader knows that there is some similarity in the metaphor and enjoys the process of figuring it out: "My heart is like a singing bird. . . ."

Similarly, two things *contrasted* are always alike. Otherwise, there would be no point in contrasting them! Who would ever undertake to contrast a window and a piano, a poem and an egg beater, a fountain pen and a shovel? Decidedly each is unlike the other; but they are so dissimilar that there would be no *point* in contrasting them. (This matter will gain further meaning in the pages that follow.)

But having explained that much about contrast and comparison, we can go on to two questions that are probably in your mind right now: First, what about sentences X, 1, 2, and 3 when we are writing a contrast or a comparison? Perhaps you recall that earlier in the book I remarked that it is quite acceptable to use for sentence X the simple form "*A* and *B* are different" (see page 18). Then sentences 1, 2, and 3 can explain that *A* and *B* are different in three important ways, and the three respective paragraphs can go on to discuss and illustrate those three ways. Of course, since you must follow Step 5, you must take care that in *some* fashion those three ways are connected (you can't show, in accordance with Step 5, that the three are connected if in fact there is no connection there).

Or instead of saying simply that *A* and *B* are different, you may have time to figure out what is the one fundamental difference that you have in mind, of which sentences 1, 2, and 3 are aspects. For instance, I could say simply that college is different from high school and then go on to give as sentences 1, 2, and 3 the facts that in college a greater quantity of work is required, a higher quality of work is required, and less help is given by the professor. Or instead, I could see all those three facts combined under the heading of maturity. Then my sentence X could read "College demands greater maturity than high school." My sentences 1, 2, and 3 could assert that it requires an amount of work, a kind of work, and an independence in work befitting the student's greater maturity.

But since *like* things are also *unlike,* and vice versa, can't we *combine* comparison and contrast in one theme? And what do we do then with sentences X, 1, 2, and 3? In sentence X we can assert that *A* and *B* are different though alike; then devote sentence 1 to the resemblance and sentences 2 and 3 to the differences. Or, naturally, we can assert that *A* and *B* are alike, though different; in the first paragraph we can discuss the difference, then in the subsequent paragraphs the likenesses.

Some students reasonably ask whether, in a theme of, say, contrast, they can't do either of those two things: make a number of individual contrasts of one kind in the first paragraph, a number of a second kind in the second paragraph, and so forth; or devote one paragraph to certain qualities of *A,* then another paragraph to the *contrasting* qualities of *B?*

An experienced reader of this book will already have the answer: the question is so reasonable that it answers itself. And the answer is *yes.* Our sole purpose is to be clear, and surely either procedure will be clear to the reader. And if the student asks "Which shall I use?" the answer is that whichever seems natural to him will probably seem natural to the reader, too. But I would add two precautions.

First, do not make a number of *individual* points about *A* in one paragraph and then give the *matching* points about *B* in the next. The result will be that the reader will have to keep glancing up and down from one paragraph to another to keep track of the various differences. This device of contrasting the material in one paragraph with that in another serves best when there are only two opposite assertions, each developed with the details that match *it,* with no attempt to match one set of details with the opposite set of details.

For example, in one paragraph I can say that statesman A throughout his career always acted on his dread of tyranny. Then I can illustrate what I've said by giving a few events in his career. Then in the next paragraph I can say that statesman B throughout his career always acted on his dread of anarchy (an opposite of tyranny, you understand: one is too much control, and the other, none). Then I can go on to illustrate what I've asserted about *B* with events from *his* career. But naturally, the *events* in *B*'s career won't be matched up with those in *A*'s. Statesman A, in fact, may have been a cabinet minister and statesman B a leading figure in a parliament, so that the events in their political lives will all be of somewhat different kinds. So the reader will not be called on to keep looking up from the second paragraph to see how the *details* match those in the first, for they won't match, of course.

The second precaution is that you must not end up with a two-paragraph theme. I hope I am not sacrificing principle to expediency in saying that the only trouble is that a two-paragraph theme, even a theme of good length, does not look like (or *feel* like) a *theme.* Well, what do you do? We can hardly demand that all twins be triplets. In fact, there *is* something *twofold* in the very nature of a comparison or contrast.

What I would do is this: to a contrast of the kind I've just described I would add a paragraph at the beginning, briefly establishing the similarity that gives the contrast its point. Both *A* and *B* were nineteenth-century statesmen, both had experienced revolution followed by reaction, and so forth. Alternately—and this is much harder—I would add a paragraph at the end making some *point* about the contrast I had written: the contrast between *A* and *B* has had other counterparts in history (name some—Jefferson and Hamilton); it seems naturally inevitable that events will always call to the fore statesmen with the opposite tendencies that are found in *A* and *B.* Mind you, to write such a concluding paragraph is harder: one runs the dangers in a conclusion of being juvenile, artificial, or obvious ("Thus we see that *A* and *B* were as different as night and day").

Assignment

First, restudy this chapter, with particular attention to the five rules of contrast. Then compare, contrast, or compare *and* contrast one of these pairs: two characters in a story (or one in one story, the other in another); two students you know (do not make up details for this comparison, much less make up imaginary students); two relatives of yours; two instructors; two kinds of manufacturing procedure; two ways of bringing up children; two periods in history; or whatever other pair you feel you can do well.

THE ARGUMENTATIVE THEME

Many if not most themes tend toward the argumentative. True, I suppose that if a physicist set out to explain to us the nature of the laser, he might involve in his paper no tinge of argument. But most of us are asserting in our themes something that we can (and perhaps do) imagine could conceivably be objected to or denied. Isn't that what we saw T. H. Huxley doing? Or at least we pretend that we may not be believed or that some readers may in effect disagree about the importance of the point we are troubling to make.

This is all to the good. For in discussing Step 4, you recall, I showed you how to steal from the fiction writer's bag of tricks; and besides the specific details you learned to adopt then, you ought now to take over *conflict.* The fiction writer uses it everywhere; besides keeping readers in doubt generally and making them wonder how things will turn out, he knows that the chief device for engaging their attention is any and every kind of conflict. When a short story opens, it may be with an argument (conflict) over who will do the dishes; or Mary Jane wants to go out, but her father expresses reluctance to let her (conflict); but somebody is usually at odds with somebody over something. And conflict continues throughout the story.

Conflict in the form of argument gives tension to a theme and endows it with a very legitimate interest that sharpens readers' awareness of the points being made. (Even contrast, which we have just studied, wins a share in this kind of interest because, in posing one thing against another, it at least imitates conflict. Art majors can tell us how this same principle operates in art, and music majors how it works in music.)

We are, therefore, interested in argument or conflict of some sort as a principle useful in nearly all themes. But we call argumentative those themes that expressly seek to persuade or convince. Now I am not going to teach you the art of persuasion; that is a higher study. But I am going to stress a few fundamentals of argumentative writing that beginning writers commonly overlook.

First, of course, you have to continue to deal with your natural tendency to be strong on asserting your ideas and weak on backing them up with reasons, examples, and facts. So review in your mind Step 4. You have learned it; you have had practice in it; but you must continue to apply it consciously, for your natural tendency will continue to be opposite to it.

For instance, perhaps you are arguing that capital punishment should be restored in your state. Since most of your friends, it seems, agree with you, you feel you have in a sense won your argument before you have even begun. But that does not mean that your argument in itself is a good one (there was a time when most people favored witch burning). For it will not do to berate the Supreme Court or to make dramatic references to notorious crimes. No, you must give your *reasons* for calling for the return of the penalty.

You start by saying that capital punishment is a deterrent to murder. Now you must say *why* you say so. "It stands to reason," you say? No; that is only theory, and theory must be submitted to test. What are the facts? You say that convicted burglars and robbers now in prison assert that in their day, when there was a death penalty, that penalty was all that deterred them from shooting the liquor store proprietor they were robbing or shooting the policeman who appeared on the scene? Now your zeal to prove that the death penalty is desirable may cause you to think that what those burglars and robbers assert also stands to reason. But to an intelligent and skeptical reader what they say may seem improbable; moreover, the reader wants not more theory—yours or the criminal's—but facts. What do the statistics show about armed crime and murder? Is there less of it (or has the increase been smaller) in states that retain the death penalty than in states that gave it up? Or the reverse? In other words, apart from what criminals *say,* what did criminals actually *do?*

If you don't know the answers to those and other relevant questions, you are hardly prepared to argue one way or the other on this issue. To have strong feelings about the death penalty and then to cast about for any plausible reasons to support your feelings is not really argument, you know. At best, it is childishness; at worst, trickery. Our feelings should be governed by the facts; we should not look only for facts that seem to justify our feelings. And, in any case, the intelligent and skeptical reader whom we must imagine as the reader of our argumentative paper is going to insist on sufficient relevant *facts*—and on logical reasoning from those facts.

Get it out of your head that any such reader is interested in your theories or in any of the theorizing that has led you to those theories (or that you have contrived in order to support them). He is interested only in the *facts* that support your theories—not ideas or "arguments."

The government ought simply to print more money and distribute it to the poor? You can argue until you're blue in the face, but what your intelligent and skeptical reader will want to know is whether, in fact, governments have ever tried such a thing and if so what have been the results.

Perhaps what has been said so far has convinced you that you had better not select argumentative topics that demand research unless you are prepared to do the research. Do not make up facts! Students should have a greater voice in governing their high schools? You realize that the intelligent and skeptical reader will want to know where, actually, students have been given such a voice and what the results have been. But do not make up a school, a plan, or a set of results! That would be dishonest, both a lie and a shirking of the assignment.

I hope you don't feel that in the paragraphs that follow I'm wandering too far off the subject of argumentative themes. Right now, the point I have in mind about the made-up theme just discussed—a point to which I will give a broad application—is this: first, to *make up* a relative, a professor, a student, a school, a business deal—anything—for an argumentative or any other kind of theme is not nearly so useful as selecting a real relative, a real professor, and so forth. One reason is that pinning oneself down to a given set of circumstances is always artistically sound: the circle for Rubens, the sonnet form for Keats. (I'd have to write a whole chapter to explain that—please just take my word for it). Another reason is that dealing with unyielding realities is always harder and hence better practice. Still another reason is that dealing with realities is a good exercise in facing the facts of life and in keeping ourselves honest. But the main reason for choosing realities is that in your other classes and in your business or professional work, you are not going to be called on for any make-believe; it is always unyielding realities that you will be dealing with, so it is those you need practice with.

For, as I've said before, it cannot be too often repeated to you, nor too heavily emphasized, that *what you write in English class is mere practice; it is what you write outside English class that is of real importance.*

You know, my fellow English professors have sometimes remarked how often, when they are introduced as English professors, people say, "Oh, I'll have to watch my English!" Not at all; English professors are as much used to errors as doctors are to sore throats. It is other people, not English professors, in whose presence you must watch your English: clients, customers, employees, employers, supervisors, subordinates. *Their* judgment will be harsh; and a *he don't* or a series of misspellings may do you damage with them.

Similarly, I've had occasion to notice that often students who write very well in their themes will then write letters, notes, memoranda, signs, even advertisements that are miserably composed and full of careless errors. Those students have the facts of life backwards! English is not something you do in English class; it is the language you speak and write hourly in your workaday life—to your credit or discredit, and with results favorable or unfavorable to you. Thus writing in English class is only preparation; your very best writing must be in your history, sociology, and anthropology classes and in your business or profession.

That is why, when a young police officer I was teaching told me after class one day that for the first time a judge had praised an arrest report he had written, I felt better satisfied than if I had learned that a former student of mine had completed a novel. For as I have said before, almost no students are going to be professional writers, yet nearly all of them will have to write. And if I can really teach all those students how to do the writing they will in fact have to do and at the same time persuade them that lessons in writing are to be applied *outside* English class, I'll feel perfectly satisfied.

But I must return to the point where I left off, when I was dealing specifically with argumentation. I was remarking, as you recall, that you should not choose such subjects as capital punishment unless you are prepared to do the research needed to form a theory. If you are not prepared to do such research, you had better choose to argue the proposition that the man next door ought to give up drinking; for you already know about the lost job, the broken leg, and the bruised child.

You can argue that proposition if you have imagination and knowledge enough to present both sides—the side of the man next door as well as your side. And I say this for two reasons. The first reason is that, as some students fail to realize, there *must* be another side; otherwise you haven't got an argument, you've got an explanation (exposition) plain and simple—that is, a sermon. Some students mistakenly pick an argumentative topic like "We should drive safely," for example. Now is there another side to that question? Is there anybody in his right mind who would assert that we should *not* drive safely?

"Well," you may say, "at least there are many people who drive recklessly." I see. And you are going to preach them a sermon on safe driving. On the one hand, remember that I have cautioned you against writing sermons—against writing on what *should be* rather than on what *is*—since that is not the kind of practice you need. But on the other hand, you should recognize that for a proposition like "We should drive safely," you don't have a real other side, and hence you don't have the makings of an argumentative theme. So finally, unless you can present a real and attractive case for your neighbor's continuing to put away a fifth a day after his drinking has led to the crumpled fender, the broken leg, and the battered child (*he* has reasons, obviously, or he wouldn't continue), then you had better choose still another topic.

The second reason is a principle that students readily understand but feel that they can get by with ignoring. (So a teacher assigning argumentative themes for the first time can usually expect them to be poor; and perhaps the only thing he can do is assign *F*'s to the papers and tell the students they have one more chance to pay real attention to the principle in a second assignment.) The principle is that *the worth of your argumentative paper depends fundamentally on how forcibly you present the other side of the question and how well you then deal with that other side.*

Yes, a student argues for disarmament without, sometimes, even mentioning the claims of those who accept the arms race so long as the United States can be in the lead in it. If he does mention those claims, he usually presents them in so poor a light that we're evidently expected to suppose that only mental defectives or madmen espouse them. But what will an intelligent and skeptical reader think if a writer neglects or slights the other side?

He will say: "Either this writer does not realize how strong the arguments on the other side are—in which case he should not be arguing—or else he is dishonestly covering up opposing claims. In any case," he will continue, "I want to see the opposing claims dealt with, for only a writer who can refute them can prove his case and convince me."

In other words, if you cannot deal with the fact that an airplane can fly upside down, you cannot prove Vernoulli's principle (according to which it can't). If you cannot deal with the fact that Russia, starting about neck and neck economically and socially with Latin America, has in about fifty years moved immeasurably ahead of it, then you certainly cannot prove that communism is less successful than free enterprise. If you cannot deal with the fact that only unimmunized people contract polio, you cannot successfully argue that all disease is psychosomatic or that germs are simply scavengers rather than pathogens. If you cannot deal with the weight of contrary critical opinion, you cannot impressively argue that Dante was a greater poet than Shakespeare.

Note: *deal with.* It is not enough to just present counterclaims; you must *refute* the other side to the satisfaction of your readers. "I don't think so" is not an argument. And I need not tell you that it will not be enough to argue that those who dispute you are crackpots or atheists, or that they are unpatriotic or subversive or "the cause of all the trouble we're having," or that they are dishonest, or that they are up to no good. If Mr. Jones maintains that both employment and unemployment are spirals, the question is not whether Jones is a Communist, a compulsive gambler, a wife beater, a provoker of street riots, a racist, or a moron; the question is strictly whether employment and unemployment are in fact spirals or in fact not.

A third matter about argumentation is of another kind, though it is connected with the presentation of the other side of the question; for it, you can review what has been said earlier on such connectives as *true . . . but.* For you must present the other side of the question (or a random objection); yet your readers must be able to see instantly that it *is* the other side, not yours (or that it *is* an objection, not part of the point *you* are making). Sometimes, of course, the arguments on the other side are true; then your signal to readers that you are presenting the other side of the question will be an introductory expression like *true, I grant, granted, admittedly, of course, naturally,* or even *now.*

Sometimes, however, you will think that the arguments on the other side are erroneous, in which case you will of course not introduce them with an expression like *true.* You will, instead, use an expression like *Marxists contend, some people believe, students sometimes mistakenly assert, it has been falsely claimed, once it was believed,* or *there are those who declare.* But in either case you must use *some* connective; otherwise your reader is liable to become quite confused.

Equally important if your reader is not to become confused is a signal to him that you have finished (at least for the time being) with presenting the other side and have now come back to argue on your own side. The very best signal for this purpose is the word *but* (though *however* will also do well for this purpose). Immediately after the word *but* you must show (a) that arguments on the other side, though true, do not destroy your argument; or (b) that arguments on the other side are false (or at least unproved).

Thus, to use very brief examples, "*Some critics contend* that we study poems to learn about life. *But* it should be clear that we study poems to learn about poems, just as we study Chopin's waltzes to learn about waltzes—not about life. For poetry is a *part* of life, just as music is." Or "*Lay people often believe* that you can help the mentally distressed at least by being willing to listen to them. *But* psychiatrists warn us that if the mentally distressed are giving voice to their illusions, we are allowing them to reinforce those illusions by giving them an opportunity to express them."

A fourth matter of concern in argumentation is the arrangement of your facts. Of course, sentence X must be an assertion of the point you are arguing: "Psychiatrists are best able to deal with our mental and emotional problems"; "Our schools need centralized rather than local control"; "Learned Hand should have been appointed to the United States Supreme Court." Next, your sentences 1, 2, and 3 (I'm assuming you're writing a short theme) can be assigned any order convenient to you and your readers (it will be an order largely dictated by the subject you are handling, of course). Sentence 1 could assert that you have evidence or proofs to offer, and paragraph 1 could offer them; paragraph 2 could present the case for the other side; and paragraph 3 could then present your handling of the other side. (Your final sentence should contain some reaffirmation of your original contention in sentence X.)

As for the order of your arguments, if you have several, put your second best *first,* your very best *last,* and the rest in between. Given five arguments, the ideal arrangement would in fact be (1) second best, (2) fifth best, (3) fourth best, (4) third best, and (5) best. That arrangement may be a little hard to remember; if you are using several arguments, you'd better have this page open before you while you're writing your theme.

Finally—and I'm afraid this most important point is the hardest for students actually to realize and make their own—remember, always remember, that we argue not to win an argument, but to get at the truth. To win an argument without having won the *truth* for yourself and others is an empty victory indeed. It's like winning a sweepstakes and finding you've won only play money. Cultivate the habit—*win* for yourself the attitude—of being pleased to see your opponent win if he is right, and always be prepared to recognize when he *is* right. After all, if you have won your argument that the capital of the United States lies farther south than any European capital (it doesn't; Lisbon and Athens are more southerly), what does that make you? No, there is no particular glory in having won an argument. There is genuine glory, instead, in possessing the truth. Whether it is won by you or by your opponent, in the end it is possessed by both of you. Truth is at once your greatest glory and your best friend. Strive for it above everything.

Assignment

Here are some exercises that your instructor will probably not want you to do all in the same day.

1. Go to the library and leaf through a number of articles in magazines like the *New Republic, Commonweal,* the *Christian Century, Commentary, Harper's,* and the *Atlantic.* Look for about half a dozen instances of arguments of the *true . . . but* or *it is claimed . . . but* variety. Your instructor may be able to give you some help with this exercise.

2. In a newspaper find an editorial (or two) that is an argument. See how it conducts the business of arguing.

3. Write an argumentative theme. To avoid the many pitfalls that have been pointed out to you in this chapter, perhaps your most honest, most successful, and best supported argument will be one you actually had *with yourself.* Mind you, I say honest. Describe a choice over which you really debated and had some difficulty making up your mind on; a choice about which you actually weighed arguments on both sides (not just changed feelings for no well-defined reason). If you never had such a debate with yourself, ignore this suggestion; don't write about your choice between

taking a job and going to college or between dropping out of high school and getting your diploma if actually there was no question whether you'd go to college or stay in high school. For we want this theme to be, above all, an exercise in trying to establish the *truth.*

EXPRESSION

There are those for whom good writing means good expression: the richness of a full vocabulary expressively used; the wit of an always right, yet constantly unexpected choice of expression; terse yet euphonious language, with everything pleasingly yet correctly placed; the spell cast by a phrasing in which suitable rhythms sustain haunting melodies and harmonious consonants sound with echoing vowels; the continually refreshing novelty of original yet unobtrusive figures of speech, of a tone firmly sustained amid a hundred variations; the charm of luminous clarity in union with subtlety and nuance, satisfying yet piquing the mind; the challenge of incongruity, irony, understatement, and paradox; the interplay of rhapsody and epigram; full choir and lone voice, freedom and restraint, magic and authority, wildwood and trimmed garden, and, in a word, the impression produced by taste and judgment directing all the forces of artful utterance that flatter the ear while they delight the sense.

That's fine, if the reader is up to it. But isn't expression good if, and only if, the reader will understand it? Otherwise, since Greek is even

176

more expressive than English, why not write Greek? No, better to be plain and correct than eloquent and misunderstood; better to be art-less where art would not be clear; better to be ugly where beauty would be less effective; better to limp into eternal life than stride into everlasting perdition.

Fine expression is fine, too, if you were born with the gift for it and have had leisure to develop it. Otherwise, you will get along without it. Thousands of charming literary vignettes lie unread while millions of mail order catalogs satisfy their readers because they tell clearly, in plain and simple English, what the merchandise is (and likewise the instructions accompanying the merchandise tell in foolproof language how to assemble it). More to the point, some students' fine talents of expression are squandered on disorganized generalities that cannot compete with themes that, though they are impoverished in vocabu-lary and uninspired in phrasing, have their clearly discernible point solidly supported and their material well connected throughout.

Good expression, therefore, can be—and often is—overvalued. By itself it certainly does not make good writing (any more than good ideas, by themselves, do). In fact, good expression can be dispensed with, and an effort to achieve it had better be dispensed with whenever the writer is straining to be impressive or to be interesting. You know what impression people produce when they speak in an unnatural voice, don't you? I cannot believe that you would want to produce a similar impression in your themes!

Still, good expression *is* good. If it is not beyond the understanding of one's intended readers, it is a fine addition to good writing. In fact, when it does what it should do—make the writer's intention and attitude clearer—it plays an integral part in good writing. So if you have powers of expression, you are to be congratulated. But what if you haven't?

Well, fortunately you can still achieve a modest degree of acceptable expression. How? By reading a lot, writing a lot, and observing a few rules.

Let's take reading first. It's your only contact with written English, after all. You can no more hope to express yourself well in written English without considerable reading than you could hope to talk easily with your friends if you seldom heard English spoken and got almost all your knowledge of English from books. But studying *this* book will not make a reader of you. That's up to you. Given that you agree that reading is good for you (and I'm aware that some teachers, even in our better high schools, quietly discourage students from reading), then I can make four suggestions that may prove helpful.

First, find (perhaps with the help of a librarian) the kind of books that interest *you.* Then read them. It doesn't matter what they are, for something is better than nothing. Second, agree with yourself that you will spend *some* time each day reading, and do not go to bed without having spent that time with a book. What time can you give? Five minutes a day? All right; five minutes is better than none. To those who scoff at this answer, let me reply that right now I am learning a new foreign language (Romanian) by applying myself carefully to the textbook for five minutes a day (including review). After just a few months I've made gratifying progress, and I am in fact a fourth of the way through the book! Five minutes is a good deal more than nothing.

Third, think of the children you are going to have or already do have. If they see you reading, they'll probably become readers; if they don't, they probably won't read. Just set a good example, and your children will automatically follow it, to their immense benefit. In other words, I would like to see you become a reader not only for your own sake but also for your children's.

Fourth, if you have some real difficulty in reading, see whether in your school, or in a nearby school, there is a reading course—perhaps as part of an adult education program. If your eye movements, for example, are wrong, the instructors in such a course may be able to correct them; if you read more slowly than normal, they may be able to show you how to increase your speed. For it would be too bad if a correctable disability kept you from joining the ranks of educated people (who have at least one thing in common: they read).[1]

Next, writing: you are going to acquire ease in written expression only through writing, just as you will only become a tennis player through playing tennis. So besides the writing you *have* to do, you might begin writing letters to someone who likes to get letters (few people do not), or you might keep a notebook in which you frequently record your thoughts and the reasons for those thoughts. Letters, by the way, are more informal than themes; yet you can help yourself by applying to your letters some of the things you have learned here. For instance, you can use topic sentences often; and going into specific detail is surely better than chewing on your pen and wondering, "What else can I say?"

In a letter to me, one of my nieces, age nine, wrote four sentences: one told me that she had had a ballet recital; another that she had had a birthday party; the third that she had been sick and home from school a day; and the last that she couldn't think of anything more to tell me. In teaching composition I have often thought of that letter and of my reflection at the time that three things were *a lot* to tell me—and would have made a full-length letter if, as she would learn to do later, she had *gone into detail* about the ballet recital, the birthday party, and even about the day's absence.

And last, the few simple rules that will make up the bulk of this chapter. I'll begin with *correctness,* since it's fundamental. And let me say first that if (though you do not say *thunk* for *thought* or *his'n* for *his*) you do say—and even write—*for she and I, who have came,* or *without hardly trying,* you have a problem the seriousness of which you obviously do not realize.

I'll have to let you take that up with your instructor or with some

---

[1]Many students have improved their reading with the help of P. Joseph Canavan and William O. Heckman, *The Way to Reading Improvement* (Boston: Allyn and Bacon, 1966).

other reliable person, however, for I cannot undertake to teach you the basic elements of usage here. All I can do is urge you to consider these points: first, apparently you have set a limit on how far you ought to go in using acceptable English. That is, you won't use *I thunk,* but neither will you bother your head much about whether it's *I have saw* or *I have seen.* The trouble is that it's not your limit that's going to count, but somebody else's. Your employer, for instance, may not mind if you say *lays awhile* for *lies awhile.* But if you say *has came* or *has saw* he may decide that he can't have you dealing with important customers or supervising other employees (who may not, because of your poor English, respect you). That's the limit *he* sets, and it's the one that counts.

Second, let's face it, the English spoken by your parents may well have proved adequate for them. But if it is not the English of those whom you plan to be associated with in the business or professional world, it is not going to be adequate for you. If your parents ridicule you for saying *I did it* instead of *I done it,* as *they* do, that's too bad. And if your closest friends ridicule good English, that's too bad. But you can't have it both ways, can you? An engineering firm is going to be slow to hire an engineer who says *I done it.* Face it.

Third, what about your own children? Are you, by your example, going to teach them to say *I done it?* Quite a nice gift to the children, isn't it?

Fourth, if you can have an instructor or someone else point out your bad errors to you, attack them one by one, systematically. You won't have many of them, but they'll be errors with words you use several times each day. The first two weeks, for instance, concentrate on *not* saying *I didn't see nobody, I didn't find nothing;* the next two weeks, on not saying *I've went.* This is work *you* have to do. There is no magic formula, and no one can follow you around all day to correct you.

But now let's suppose that though you, like the majority of other Americans, say *the book is laying on the table,* your English is pretty acceptable. What then?

Well, if you really want your usage to be nearly faultless, go to the library and get the books on usage and go through each systematically, finding the errors you make—and learning, of course, to correct them. There you will learn to use *in the circumstances* instead of *under the circumstances; the consensus* instead of *the consensus of opinion; provided* instead of *providing; vale of tears* instead of *veil of tears;* and so on, almost without end.

Meanwhile, I have a much shorter list right here, comprising the errors and weaknesses in usage, punctuation, and coherence, that I find most frequently today in themes (and in print) and that I view at the same time as serious enough to demand your attention. Study this list and you will begin to be more aware of correctness in expression.

NOTES ON CORRECT EXPRESSION

above, below Although dictionaries seem to allow it, do not use the words *above* and *below* to refer to parts of your papers. Use *preceding* or *foregoing* and *following: the preceding paragraph, the following paragraph.* (What if what you refer to as *above* ends up at the bottom of the page when you type your paper?)

all of Means "the whole of." Do not use to mean "all" (do not say "The first customer bought all of my plants")!

amount Do not use with plurals; use *number: amount of paper, number of pieces of paper.*

and others, etc. Do not use *and others* or *etc.* in formal writing. Too often students resort to these expressions when they cannot think of enough examples.

area, level You had better use these words only in the physical sense ("What is the *level* of the water today?" "How do you find the *area* of a circle?"). "She teaches on the college level" for "She teaches college" and "She teaches in the English area" for "She teaches English" are unnecessarily wordy. Like "She is effective in the classroom situation" for "She is effective in the classroom" (I would say simply "She is a good teacher"), they suggest that the speaker or writer is straining to sound professional.

as far as Say either "*as far as* I know" or "*as far as* use by our firm goes." Do *not* say "As far as use by our firm, I don't think we need it."

as to Like *in terms of,* this is sometimes a lazy way of finding the right preposition *(questions as to his age* for *questions about his age)* or a falsely elegant padding *(the question as to whether she eloped* for *the question whether she eloped).* Avoid *as to* except when you are turning to another aspect of a topic ("Now *as to* the speaker's third point, I think. . . .").

class   Vulgar when used to mean "good quality." *Classy* is even worse.

due to   Avoid this expression if you can. Technically *due,* since it's an adjective, must go directly with a person or with a thing. So "Her absence *was due* to sickness" is correct, because you have a thing, *absence,* that was due to sickness. But "She was absent due to sickness" is incorrect, because there's no person or thing in that sentence that's *due* to sickness. Some dictionaries accept *due to sickness* as a colloquial word (acceptable in speech but not in writing); but be safe and avoid using *due to* whenever you can.

facet   Stay out of trouble by using *facet* only when you are speaking of jewels.

he, she   Do not say "A student may turn in two themes if he or she wishes." *He* alone includes both sexes in such sentences, as does the word *man* when it is used to mean "mankind." (The same is true for the word *his.*)

hopefully   This word is often misused, even by the best writers. Be safe and avoid it.

–ing   A verb ending in *-ing* or beginning with *to,* except when it is used as a noun (*"Dancing* tires me"; *"To know* her is *to love* her") must be preceded or followed by the person or thing that is performing the action. "Sitting in this chair, there is a cold draft"—who is sitting? The draft? "Sitting in this chair, *I* feel a cold draft" is correct. Sometimes you can switch to passive voice to avoid this error. For example, "The paper can be moistened by dipping it momentarily in water" can be corrected to read "The paper can be moistened by *being dipped* momentarily in water."
   Do not use the words *so, as, how, very, too, more, most, less,* or *least* directly before an *-ing* word, the past participle of a verb *(connected, taught),* or a prepositional phrase *(on my side, in the hall).* You *cannot* say, for example, *very ravaging, less connected,* or *more on my side,*

because things are either ravaging or not ravaging, connected or not connected, on my side or not on my side. There is no in-between. (If a dictionary lists an -*ing* word or a third principal part as an *adjective,* you *may* use *so, as,* and so forth directly before it: *very interesting, more excited.* But most careful writers do not do so.)

In general (though there are exceptions), do not use the word *with* with an -*ing* expression. *With him following along* and *with Jones being the backup man* are poor style. Revise, getting rid of eitr the *with* or the -*ing* word: *with him behind us, with Jones as the backup man.*

less   Do not use with plurals; use *fewer: less paper, fewer pieces of paper.*

mannerism, usage   See a dictionary for these two words. They are not, as you might think, high-class substitutes for *use* and *manner;* they are very different in meaning. "He has nice mannerisms" is grotesque.

media   This word—like *phenomena, data,* and *stigmata*—is plural. You cannot say "This media is expanding." You must say "This *medium (phenomenon, datum, stigma)* is expanding." I myself never have to talk about media. Why do you? It's like the word *environment.* I don't know that I have ever used it; but students seem to have to use it in every other theme (and almost invariably they misspell it).

Miss, Mr., Mrs.   Never put a title of any kind *before* your own signature. And ordinarily, do not use titles before the name of a character in fiction or the name of an author.

–ness   Avoid words ending in -*ness* unless they are commonly used (*goodness, fairness*) or a substitute won't fit. I used the awkward words *interestingness* and *impressiveness* earlier in this book because in the place I used them, many of my readers would have misunderstood *interest* and *impression.* But ordinarily, do not use *evilness* for *evil, beautifulness* for *beauty, decentness* for *decency, industriousness* for *industry,* or *indifferentness* for *indifference.*

not   We are told by authorities on expression not to use the word *not* when we can avoid it, except in the expression *not . . . but.* In somewhat the same spirit of bravado with which Dr. Samuel Johnson brushed aside a concern for keeping one's underwear clean, let me say that I generally disregard this rule. But if you can form the habit of using other negatives instead of *not,* or of substituting positive expressions, you will improve your writing ("This rose *has no* thorns" instead of "This rose *does not have* thorns"; "The door *is shut*" for "The door is not open"). But neither strain to avoid *not* nor falsify your meaning; and before you adopt this whole rule about *not* simplistically, read Shakespeare's Sonnet 116.

noun modifiers   Do not use a noun to modify a noun when you can use an adjective instead. That is, do not write *education policies;* write *educational policies.* Use prepositional phrases when you can to avoid too many pairings of nouns: *difficulties with transportation* instead of *transportation difficulties.* Noun modifiers tend to work well only when short, familiar household words are involved: *mouse hole, rabbit meat, grass seed, light bulb.*

passed away   Use *died* instead.

past participles   See **-ing.**

peers, siblings   Except in technical papers, these words are incorrect for *playmates, schoolmates, associates, fellows,* and *brothers* or *sisters.*

portray   It is easy to overuse or misuse this word, so be safe and avoid it.

possessives   You will be safest if you use the *-'s* and *-s'* forms only for people and never for things. That is, you can write *men's clothing,* since men are people; but do not write "Clothing's life depends on the care taken of it," for clothing is not a person. Write *the life of clothing.* True, there are many cases in which *-'s* is perfectly acceptable: "Hark, hark, the lark at *heaven's* gate sings." But be on the safe side and write *the gate of heaven.*

prepositional phrases   See **-ing.**

quotation   Do not use the informal *quote* to mean "quotation." (In printers' technical language, *quotes* is used to mean "quotation marks.")

Do not refer to something as a *quotation* (much less as a *quote*) simply because *you* have quoted it. Say *the preceding line (passage, paragraph, statement),* not *the preceding quotation,* unless the person you are quoting is quoting someone else.

quotation marks   Do not use quotation marks to indicate slang, nicknames, or other informal usage. The quotation marks used below are incorrect.

> He was "crazy" about her.
> She has a "neat" way of talking.
> He was never sent to "Nam."
> He played the "sax" in our "combo."

Choose either to use a word or not to use it; don't feel that you take the curse off a bad word by decorating it with quotation marks. No, using quotation marks in that way, you only make yourself look foolish. (An American writer, Ring Lardner, I think, cruelly made fun of a character in one of his stories exactly by having her enclose words within quotation marks frequently in her letters.) Sometimes, it is true, there seems no way out of this use; so a rare instance is permissible—say once in three themes. But the use I have warned you against is a vicious habit, and you must not let it get out of hand.

Always put commas and periods within (before) quotation marks. Put other marks of punctuation inside only if they are part of what you are quoting.

When you use quotation marks to indicate titles of stories and poems, do not use commas as well; that is, do not say:

> Yeats wrote, "Among School Children," in 1927.

Take out the commas. This is an error that most students make.

Though in this book we are not concerned with the research paper, I should nevertheless mention that in your paper (except for dialogue, of course) quoted matter over two lines long should (a) have no quotation marks around it but (b) be indented at the left (when you are typing, do *not* single-space such quoted material). For example, if I want to quote Francis Bacon on lack of concentration, I do it this way.

Bacon, in his essay "On Studies," says:
> So if a man's wit be wandering, let him study the mathematics; for in demonstrations, if his wit be called away never so little, he must begin again.

semicolon   Make it a rule never to use a semicolon where you could *not* use a period instead. It's easy to make mistakes with semicolons otherwise.

somewhat   Say *something of a failure,* not *somewhat of a failure.*

state (verb)   Use only to mean "put into words" ("*State* your idea in the first sentence") or "declare formally and authoritatively" ("The President has *stated* to Congress that he will veto the bill"). Do not use as a synonym for *say, write,* or *assert;* "Shakespeare states that the course of true love never did run smooth" is comical.

that   Avoid using a comma in place of *that* (not "My misfortune is, I cannot read rapidly," but "My misfortune is *that* I cannot read rapidly"). The omission of *that* is a tricky construction that could trip you up; writing *that* is easier and more natural for most students.

Repeat the word *that* in parallel constructions: "He asserted *that* he had missed the meeting and they would have to get the information elsewhere" should read "and *that* they would have to get the information elsewhere." (*Because, if,* and all other subordinating conjunctions must also be repeated in most parallel constructions.)

Do not use *that of* in an unnecessary or illogical manner. "His tie is longer than that of James" is unnecessarily complicated; "His tie is longer than James's" is much better. (If you have trouble with apostrophes, get a good grammar handbook and refer to it frequently.) But sentences like "The ordinary freight train in the thirties was shorter than that of the ordinary freight train today" are totally illogical; omit *that of!*

the   Among the signs of the inexperienced writer is the overuse (actually, misuse) of the word *the.* When you correct your written work, go through it one last time to see how many *the*'s you can either cross out or replace with *a, an, this,* or some other word. Take, for example, this sentence: "That year the dream sequences featured in the dance films were also used in the cartoon films, which were much like the dance films in the free use of the plot." Every *the* in that sentence can be—and should be—taken out. (To see what I mean, cross out every *the* and reread the sentence.) True, you can go too far in eliminating *the.* And naturally you cannot eliminate it if the result is not English: "Artist's work is to be found in rooms of largest museum in capital city of Tuscany." But I would rather see you go too far in this elimination for a while—make it, in fact, a kind of specialty of yours—until you reach the point where you will sometimes restore a dispensable *the,* but will do so out of a conviction that it is better left in, not out of mere blind habit.

In your writing, take special care to see that if a sentence begins with *the,* the following sentence does not also begin with *the,* unless you are deliberately setting up a pattern. In fact, the word *the* used frequently at the beginning of sentences seems particularly objectionable.

to me   Use only when it fits. "*To me* he seems very old" is correct, because *seems to me* is correct. "To me he is something of a failure" is incorrect because "He is a failure to me" is not idiomatic English. Say *to my mind, to my way of thinking,* for those are good idiomatic English.

type   Do not use as a synonym for *kind* or *sort. Type* is a technical word that belongs in a technical context; it should be used only when *kind* would be wrong (for example, you must say, "What is your blood *type?*").

want   As a noun, this means "lack." Do not use it to mean "wish" or "desire."

which   Do not use to refer to people, as in *a man which I know.*

With the help of your instructor you could add hundreds of errors to this list. I no doubt have overlooked a few that I should have included. But in the main, avoid the ones I have listed here and you will avoid the worst, most frequently found, and most conspicuous blemishes that disfigure beginning writers' style.

But let's turn our attention to your whole style, saying something of consistency of tone, vocabulary, succinctness, and variety in expression. But before I turn to tone I want to insert here one rule worth all the rest together: *never try to be cute.* Even in children *conscious* cuteness is repulsive. And where humor is substituted for information or explanation, where smart-alecking takes the place of earnestness, where language directs attention to its cute self—where, in fact, cuteness is the tone—you have the worst kind of writing you can do.

CONSISTENCY OF TONE

We said something of this matter earlier; to say what should be said would take at least a long chapter. In the brief treatment of expression in this book, I can only remind you that in any single composition you should select one kind of language (formal, informal or colloquial) and stick to it. Do not refer to something as *sustenance* in one line, a *meal* in another, and *chow* in still another. Such a succession of sentences as the following is artistically faulty: "Will this terrain provide suitable sustenance for our forces? Can our men make a meal of rice? What will the boys in the chow lines say about the stuff we can get here?"

But producing a sustained tone is, after all, an art—perhaps an instinct. And certainly it cannot be produced without an adequate vocabulary, to which we will turn now.

VOCABULARY

Though you might not dream it to read this book, I have perhaps as large a vocabulary as anyone else you will ever meet, and not just in one language but in several. But I'm not sure that that makes me able to give *you* advice on building your vocabulary—any more, say, than a person six-foot-two is able to give young children tips on how to grow tall.

Still, we know that in your first half dozen years you acquired a vocabulary of several hundred words without effort, simply by exposure. So though your mind is less impressionable now than it was then, you can still acquire words by simple exposure—if you meet them often enough in the process of *regular reading.* Moreover, when you learn words through reading you learn also their *use* and their *connotations.* The dictionary, in contrast, tells you that *siblings* means brothers and sisters, but it does not tell you that our best writers never use the word. The dictionary can tell you that *eerie* means "fear-inspiring, weird, uncanny," but you will learn the full force of the word only when a novelist uses it to describe the sound of a creaking door in a deserted house standing in moonlit countryside. I find it hard to teach students of literature the connotations (the suggestions, the emotional force, the overtones) of *desolate* and *forlorn* if they are meeting them for the first time in Keats's odes—and certainly a dictionary is no help.

I don't recall that I ever had a dictionary in any language until I was in my twenties, nor a dictionary in a foreign language, except for Latin and Greek, until I was in my forties. Still, my English is not as exact as I wish you—with the help of a dictionary—would make yours. Look at the word *instance* in your dictionary and see the differences, the distinctions, the dictionary gives among *instance, example, case,* and *illustration.* These are distinctions of a kind I'm afraid I do not make; but it would be good if you (not so old a dog as I) could learn to make them. For another thing, if, because of not understanding a word, you cannot get the *point* of something you are reading, well, common sense will send you to a dictionary. (Still, if you are reading a Marxist essay and need to know the meaning there of *dialectic, alienation,* and *anomie,* you will not find the dictionary of much help.)

Again, if you are writing and are not sure of the meaning (or spelling) of a word you are about to use, you had better see what help the dictionary can give you. And by the way, you'll have to keep a dictionary right by you from the start, because experience will show you that you won't get up to get it when you need it, even if it's no farther than a few steps away.

For a different kind of help from the dictionary, begin to *notice* words. And stop occasionally to figure out, from the way a word is used, what it must mean: " 'A candidate, if unknown, will not be elected' employs an *ellipsis* of *he is* ('if *he is* unknown')." What must *ellipsis* mean in that sentence? Since *he is* is shown to be left out, doesn't it probably mean a *leaving out?*

Yet, finally, remember what I have told you before. It may be nice to know the meanings of *sciolist, congeries, endemic, factitious, irredentist, leucomelanous, seriatim,* and *lemma.* But three things occur to me when I see vocabulary enrichment of that kind. First, students' trouble in reading is not so much with words like that, but with *proper nouns,* which writers frequently use to convey their impressions: the Rosetta stone, Rorschach, Freud, the Battle of Hastings, Queen Victoria, Falstaff, Don Quixote, Alice, Uncle Tom, the Parthenon, Linnaeus, the *Beagle,* Pythagoras, Walter Mitty, Mrs. Grundy, a Judas, a Moses, the Rubicon, and all the other references that students can learn only from *diligent* application to all their courses.

Second, I'd far rather see students at home with words like *get, set, hand, foot,* and *head* than in thrall to words like *naive* (which they often misspell), *introvert,* and *participatory.*

EXPRESSION

189

Third, let me say again that the real weakness in students' vocabularies is lack of knowledge of, and use of, the little words we think with, like *therefore, thus, whereas, although, however,* and *but.* Those are the words students should start with when they attempt to improve their vocabularies.

SUCCINCTNESS

Under Step 4 we said that our aim was to write a lot about a little. Now without losing any of that "a lot," we must try to say it in as few words as we can. Why? Because words, unless they're making a real contribution to what you are saying by adding some detail, are like water added to milk, Coca-Cola, or Seven-Up. The more water you add, the weaker and less tasteful you make the milk or whatever it is you are drinking. Milk and water mixed half and half would be only half so nutritious and half so enjoyable as straight milk.

Or look at it from the opposite point of view: the more condensed something becomes, the stronger it gets. Brandy is stronger than wine because the distiller produces brandy by extracting about half the water content of the wine. Let half the water of a bottle of blue ink evaporate and the ink becomes twice as dark. And if you simmer away half the water from soup, the soup becomes twice as thick and nourishing. So if you can say something in half the number of words you originally took, what you will end up saying will be twice as forceful, twice as artistically pleasing, and twice as effective.

Again, however, as in the whole matter of expression, we must remember the reader; cutting out useless words will be of help to his understanding up to a point. But beyond that point, the more concise anything is, the more slowly and thoughtfully it has to be read and the more difficult it becomes for inexperienced readers. But at your stage in writing you will probably not become so terse as to be puzzling, and I can safely suggest to you four ways in which—without losing any details—you can save words.

The first way is simply to cut out words that don't add anything. Take as a simple example the sentence "He lives at 604 Elm Street, in a little brown house that was built by his grandfather." Study that sentence. What can you omit? Certainly not *built by his grandfather,* for that adds information. And I must make it clear that we are not judging here the *value,* the *importance,* the *necessity* of any information—that is quite another matter; we are trying to preserve *all* the information, of whatever kind, yet reduce the number of words. What about *brown?* It doesn't add much, you say. But it adds *something,* so keep it.

I wonder whether you have discovered that we can omit two words—*that was*—yet leave the whole meaning intact: "He lives at 604 Elm Street, in a little brown house built by his grandfather." Study this example until you see clearly that (a) two words have been omitted, but (b) no idea has been omitted (not even any that you consider valueless or unnecessary).

Now not only does this revised sentence serve as an example of the process of cutting out words that add nothing; it provides a clue to one very useful rule for terseness: whenever a *relative pronoun (who, whose, whom; which; what; that)* is followed by a part of the verb *to be (am, is, are; was, were; will be; has been, have been; be, being, been)* simply remove both the relative pronoun and the verb, unless what remains is awkward or changes your meaning.

Similarly, whenever the verb of a short sentence is a form of the verb *to be,* see whether it can't be removed and the remainder of the sentence grafted onto the sentence before or after it. For example: "Alfred was a scholarly king. He translated several books into English. They were of an inspirational character." This can be changed to "Alfred, a scholarly king, translated into English several books of an inspirational character" (or "several inspirational books"). If you have a special interest in writing, experiment extensively with combining sentences in this way—but don't overdo it!

The second way to shorten sentences without losing anything is *ellipsis,* the omission of repeated words. For example: "The father was a madman, the son a fool." Here we can omit *was* from *the son was a fool* because *was* is already used in *was a madman.* Another example: "The judge condemned, and the hangman hanged, a man as innocent as you or I." *A man* need not be used after *condemned* because it is stated later, after *hanged.* Two pieces of advice: first, notice ellipsis in your reading and see how (and how often) it is used. Second, try *not* to use it when you are writing for unsophisticated readers.

The third way to eliminate unneeded words is to reduce clauses to phrases and phrases to single words. For example, the clause *when the sun rises* can be shortened to the phrase *at sunrise; if it should happen to rain* to *in case of rain.* So the phrase *with tenderness* can be reduced to *tenderly; having comparatively little weight* to *light; way of pronouncing words* to *pronunciation; give birth to* to *bear;* and *an insoluble difficulty* to *an impasse.* Do not do this if what results sounds unnatural to you, however.

A fourth way of shortening sentences—a favorite of writers of action stories, you may have noticed—is to use one grammatical subject followed by several predicates: "Superspy hesitated only a fraction of a second, then tore open the door, charged into the smoke-filled room, hurled the grenade into the open safe, spun around, leaped back into the hall, and slammed the door." Here the subject, Superspy, is followed by seven predicates in the same clause: *hesitated, tore, charged, hurled, spun, leaped,* and *slammed.* Of course, you will notice that writers less obviously bursting with red corpuscles do—in less breathless prose—the same thing, seeking not drama, of course, but compactness. Thus the Roman poet Virgil, who never hurled a grenade in his life, wrote: "Others, to be sure, will more deftly beat bronze into lifelike shapes, will draw living faces from marble, will better plead cases at law, will better chart the course of the heavenly bodies, and will predict the ascent of the stars: but, O Roman, remember—for these must be your talents—you will sway people with the rod of empire, will lay upon them the customs of peace, will spare the humble, and will put down the proud" (*Aeneid* 6. 847–53). Thus Virgil says that others will beat, will draw, will plead, will chart, and will predict; you will sway, will lay, will spare, and will put down. Each of his subjects (*others* and *you*) has, thus, several predicates.

Common sense will show you that sometimes you will not want to use this procedure. As often as not, however, you will do well to apply at least the following rule, which will give you one subject followed by two predicates: when two clauses are joined by *or, and,* or *but* and the subject of the second clause is a pronoun that means the same as the subject of the first, simply omit that pronoun. *Memorize this rule and apply it whenever you can.* For example: "Illinois has a large metropolitan area, but it is also one of the most important farming states." There are two clauses: *Illinois has* and *it is* (subject, verb; subject, verb). The second subject, *it,* is a pronoun and means the same thing as the first subject, *Illinois.* The two clauses have *but* between them. I can therefore omit the pronoun *it* and say, "Illinois has a large metropolitan area but is also one of the most important farming states."

VARIETY IN EXPRESSION

Finally, it will not be enough to be correct and succinct if you do not notice in your reading, and practice in your writing, a pleasing variety in the length and arrangement of your sentences.

First let's take *length,* since it is the simplest. The rule that used to be given to students was to vary a series of long sentences with an occasional short one. Today, when students tend to write all short sentences, the rule has to be reversed: vary a succession of short sentences with an occasional long one. Practically, I should say, every third or fourth sentence should be noticeably longer than the others.

But how do you make a sentence longer? Just by adding more words? No. But I think that if you try to apply the following rule, you will have a sufficient number of longer sentences: do not put every idea in a simple little sentence of its own, but combine ideas into longer, more complex sentences. Take the following, for example.

> "The Culture of Modernism" is one of the two or three best essays in Howe's book. In that essay Howe describes modern literature. By modern literature he means the literature of the past century and a half. He shows that it tends in general toward the solipsistic, the problematic, the nihilistic.

Some of those short sentences, surely, can be combined into long ones. Why don't you try your hand at combining them? Then I'll try my own hand at it. But you do yours first before looking at mine. Well, then:

> In "The Culture of Modernism," one of the two or three best essays in the book, Howe describes modern literature—that of the past century and a half—as tending in general toward the solipsistic, the problematic, and the nihilistic.

Several revisions of this short passage are possible, and yours may well be better than mine.

What if you reduce the number of sentences required by Step 3 when you combine short sentences into long ones? Well, it's better to have fewer sentences and some variety in length than more sentences and no variety in length. You can add additional sentences with more examples or a further explanation to make up the number of sentences required by Step 3.

Variety in sentence *form* is the last matter I will treat formally here. First, let me tell you that if you are able to put into practice the rules I have given you about (a) omitting a relative pronoun followed by a form of the verb *to be* (page 191), (b) joining to the sentence after it or before it the remainder of a sentence from which you have taken out some form of the verb *to be* (page 191), and (c) combining some short sentences into longer ones (as just described in the last paragraph), you have *already* acquired three methods that tend to give variety to the form of your sentences.

But now, if you are interested in doing not just acceptable, but *good* writing, I know of no way so effective for you to learn thoroughgoing variety in your sentence patterns and to form an attractive, sophisticated, modern style than to follow the method in Joseph P. Collignon's *Patterns for Composition* (a fairly long approach through writing) or his *Sound of Prose* (a short oral approach).[2] Remember, of course, that it will do you no good simply to glance through either book, for both involve a *method,* the instructions for which you must follow step by step.

Meanwhile, you can go a long way by following the advice I gave you earlier in this book about varying the *beginnings* of your sentences. This is a simple matter of sometimes moving something from the middle or end of your sentence up to the very beginning. (But note: don't apply this method of achieving variety to either explicit references or connectives like *however.* Review pages 128 and 140 before you start to practice varying the beginnings of your sentences.)

I'll give you some examples of varied beginnings. First I'll give each sentence unrevised, with the part to be moved in italics; then the revised sentence.

These scars will *eventually* disappear.
Eventually these scars will disappear.

Witches build their houses of candy *to entice children.*
To entice children, witches build their houses of candy.

I can be in Chicago within a few hours *by taking the morning flight.*
By taking the morning flight, I can be in Chicago within a few hours.

Do a little reading *whenever there is time.*
Whenever there is time, do a little reading.

The two sticks *joined together* will just reach the window.
Joined together, the two sticks will just reach the window.

Beethoven, *a revolutionary musician in his time,* now sounds quite orthodox.
A revolutionary musician in his time, Beethoven now sounds quite orthodox.

The prospects of easy profits were *gone.*
Gone were the prospects of easy profits.

[2]Joseph P. Collignon, *Patterns for Composition* (Beverly Hills, Calif.: Glencoe Press, 1969); *The Sound of Prose* (Beverly Hills, Calif.: Glencoe Press, 1971).

Americans chewed a great deal of tobacco *in days gone by.*
In days gone by Americans chewed a great deal of tobacco.

I don't want it, *be it cheap or dear.*
Be it cheap or dear, I don't want it.

"But doesn't a person just do that kind of thing naturally?" you may ask. No. It's natural enough in itself, but as you may see in a minute, you don't *do* it without thinking about it; and as a result you'll have to keep your mind on it, either when you write or when you go over what you have written to add the finishing touches.

In fact, all I have set before you in this book is natural enough, something every instructor will insist on and that *you* ought to insist on. That your theme have a *point?* Naturally. But it won't if you don't force yourself to begin with a sentence X. That the paragraphs have topic sentences related to that point? Naturally. But they won't if you don't force yourself to write sentences 1, 2, and 3. That your general statements be backed up by generous facts and examples? Naturally. But they won't unless you deliberately set about to make them so. That your paragraphs be clearly connected with one another and that the role each sentence plays within your paragraphs be clarified by connectives? Naturally. But they won't if you don't remember to make them so.

And will your instructor, or any reader, insist that your comparisons and contrasts be properly matched up? Of course. But they wouldn't be if the need hadn't been called to your attention. That, in arguments, your assertions be backed up by facts, not by theories or predictions? Of course. But they wouldn't be if you simply didn't think about it. That your expression be minimally sophisticated? Yes. But left to grow wild, it wouldn't be.

Assignment

Finally, take as much of this chapter as you can at a time, go back through the themes you have written, and improve the expression in them. For instance, correct each misused *state* and *type.* Where you find several sentences of similar length, combine some. Where you can shorten sentences without omitting information, shorten them. Where successive sentences begin with the subject, begin one or more with something else.

Be generous with your time and attention in this assignment. It's your first step toward mastery of expression.

INDEX

O

P

Q

R

S

T

B 4
C 5
D 6
E 7
F 8
G 9
H 0
I 1
J